When I
Survey the
Wondrous Cross

When I Survey the Wondrous Cross

Scriptural Reflections for Lent

Patrick J. Ryan, S.J.

Paulist Press
New York/Mahwah, N.J.

Book and cover design by Lynn Else

Interior artwork by Charlotte Lichtblau

Library of Congress Cataloging-in-Publication Data

Ryan, Patrick J., 1939-
    When I survey the wondrous Cross : scriptural reflections for Lent / Patrick J. Ryan.
        p. cm.
    ISBN 0-8091-4207-4 (alk. paper)
    1. Lent—Prayer-books and devotions—English. 2. Catholic church—Prayer-books and devotions—English. 3. Bible—Meditations. I. Title.
    BX2170.L4R93 2005
    242′.34—dc22

                                                                2003014373

Published by Paulist Press
997 Macarthur Boulevard
Mahwah, New Jersey 07430

www.paulistpress.com

Printed and bound in the
United States of America

CONTENTS

For Mary Ryan O'Reilly
and
Liam Cathal O'Reilly

When I survey the wondrous cross

On which the Prince of glory died,

My richest gain I count but loss,

And pour contempt on all my pride.

Isaac Watts (1674–1748)

INTRODUCTION

The fifty days of the Easter season—Easter Sunday through Pentecost Sunday—constitute the oldest liturgical season known to Christians, corresponding to the interval between the Jewish Passover celebration (the Feast of Unleavened Bread) and the Feast of First Fruits (the Feast of Weeks). The early church celebrated these fifty days as one long Sunday of the resurrection, eliminating all fasting or kneeling at its liturgical celebrations from that joyful time. Only gradually did those fifty days separate the celebration of the triumph of Jesus over death from the commemoration of his ascension and the sending of the Holy Spirit on the disciples. In its origins, this season saw these three moments of the divine irruption into history as aspects of the same saving mystery. Immediately before that great celebration of the new Passover of Jesus' triumph over sin and his resurrection as the first fruits of the dead, the church started with at least one day of fasting, a day that corresponded to Holy Saturday in today's liturgical calendar. Gradually, as the fourth and fifth centuries saw the development of the church in the declining Roman Empire and beyond, the fast of Holy Saturday extended backwards, taking on the contours of the forty days Jesus spent fasting in the wilderness of Judea.

Nearly every Romance language of Europe refers to the season of Lent by some variant of its Latin name, *Quadragesima*, the "fortieth" day. English, however, designates Lent merely with the name of the season of the year to which it most closely corresponds, spring—in Old English, *lencten*, and in Middle English, *lente*. The Latin name refers to the fortieth day before the feast of Easter, just as Pentecost derives from the Greek word for the fiftieth day after the Passover celebration. The English preference for spring rather than for computation of the days of fasting commends itself as a positive approach to this season of preparation for the celebration of the dying and rising of Jesus.

Lent quickly took on a specific identity as the principal season of preparing catechumens for baptism, initiation into the life of the risen Christ. Eventually, and realistically, it also became a season of preparing repentant, already baptized Christians for reconciliation with the Lord and the church traduced by them in such major sins as apostasy, murder and adultery. Lenten fasting for forty days (during the daylight hours, and not usually including Sundays) cannot be traced much earlier than the fourth century. Compromises of the daytime fast soon developed, with the main meal working its way back from evening to 3:00 P.M. to noon, a time of day deriving its name from the anticipation of the ninth (Latin: *nona*) hour at the sixth hour of daylight. A light evening meal (originally only a beverage for monks exhausted from working in field or scriptorium) took the name of collation from the fact that it once took place during the reading of the Conferences (*Collationes*) of the Abbot Cassian (d. ca. A.D. 435). This particular relaxation of the Lenten fast only dates from the ninth century, and it is hard to imagine that the Abbot Cassian would have approved. A light breakfast, also thought of as a collation, made its appearance later in history, as well as permission to eat meat, fish and milk products.

Over the years, the relaxation of the Lenten fast has accompanied a greater emphasis on Lent as a time of preparation for initiation into the life of the church through baptism or reunification with the church through the sacrament of reconciliation. The scriptural readings for the Lenten season gradually developed in the church of the Latin rite. The readings selected over the centuries usually reflected one or another stage of the process of preparing candidates for baptism or reconciling penitents. Some of the readings reflected the Roman locale (one or another "stational" church) in which the pope, the bishop of Rome, would celebrate the sacred mysteries on that particular day. The revised Roman lectionary of 1969 adapted these readings to make them relevant as well to those who do not participate in liturgical activity in the city of Rome itself.

All of Lent may be construed as a pilgrimage through the desert into the Promised Land of Easter. Sundays in Lent, like all Sundays, share a common paschal identity with the Sundays in the Easter season. As the season of Lent progresses, the Fridays take on more of a Good Friday identity, foreshadowing the liturgical celebration of the suffering and death of Jesus. But the season is not particularly mournful, even if violet liturgical vestments predominate in liturgical haberdashery and such joyful symbolic details as the use of flowers and the elaborate musical accompaniment of the organ are limited or even discouraged during this time of the year. But the church is not in mourning for its risen Lord, even if it communally repents for the sinful behavior of its very fallible members. Accompaniment of the candidates for baptism gives all who participate in the liturgical life of the Lenten season a sense of progressing towards a goal, full incorporation into the life of Christ and his church. Not for nothing the church refers to Lent as a joyful season in the First Preface for Lent. Starting in dust and ashes, the season brings us to the possibility of seeing in the one mocked, crowned with thorns and crucified between two thieves the Lord of the living and dead.

A few of these reflections, especially for the Sundays of Lent, derive from columns I once published in *America*, the Jesuit journal of opinion, although no one appears exactly as it did originally. Many of the drawings by Charlotte Lichtblau also were first presented in that setting. I am grateful to the editors and to Charlotte Lichtblau for permission to use this material again in this setting. The scripture texts quoted in this volume all derive from the New Revised Standard Version (1989).

In the season of Lent catechumens preparing for the sacraments of initiation at Easter undergo the final stages of their catechumenate in rituals of election and scrutiny (the latter more accurately described as exorcisms) included in the celebrations of the first, third, fourth and fifth Sundays of this season. Ordinarily the readings for Cycle A should be used for communities preparing such candidates for entry into the church. Weekdays may also be used for rituals of giving the candidates for baptism the Our Father and the Niceno-Constantinopolitan Creed (the ordinary profession of faith on Sundays and solemnities). The gift of the Our Father might suitably be given on Tuesday of the first week of Lent, when Matthew's version of the Our Father is contained in the gospel reading, although at Saint Augustine's time it was only given to the candidates for baptism in the last weeks of Lent. In antiquity the Our Father was only given to the candidates after the first scrutiny (i.e., during the third week of Lent) and the creed only after the third scrutiny (i.e., during the fifth week of Lent). In that era both the Our Father and the creed were kept secret from non-Christians. The changed circumstances of modern times might argue for an earlier liturgical presentation of these two essentials of Christian life and faith. There was also, at one time in the early Roman church, a tradition of giving the candidates the Ten Commandments. This could be suitably done in the third week of Lent, perhaps on Wednesday of that week. The creed might more suitably be given at a Sunday Mass, when it is recited, perhaps on the second Sunday of Lent, when there are no scrutinies or other rites of preparation of candidates for baptism.

Chapter 1

THE FIRST FOUR DAYS OF LENT

ASH WEDNESDAY
Readings: Joel 2:12–18; 2 Corinthians 5:20–6:2;
Matthew 6:1–6, 16–18

FUNNY FACE

The association of ashes with conversion and repentance reaches back to ancient Israelite practice. The ashes of a red heifer burned as a sin offering were used by Moses and Aaron and their followers to effect ritual cleanness after ritual impurity (Num 19). Mourners in ancient Israel tore their garments and streaked their faces with ashes. In the Christian Middle Ages, a dying person might be laid on the ground on a sackcloth sprinkled with ashes as death approached. After reminding the person that "dust thou art and unto dust thou shalt return" (see Gen 3:19), the dying Christian would be asked: "Art thou content with sackcloth and ashes in testimony of thy penance before the Lord in the day of judgment?" Ideally the dying Christian responded: "I am content." Today he or she might ask for a second opinion.

Although Ash Wednesday has never achieved the dubious distinction of being called a holy day of obligation (holiday of obligation sounded too funny), many American churches find attendance more brisk than on other days so designated. No matter what your standing with God and with the church, you can always receive ashes on your forehead in the form of a cross and

resolve to do something about your life of faith and hope and charity. You may not keep up with that resolve over the forty weekdays of Lent, but an ineffectual resolve still means more than no resolve at all.

Ashes on the forehead on a winter Wednesday used to provide an easy guide to identifying Catholics in public places some years ago. Nowadays, however, there are many other Christians who bear the cruciform smudge of ashes on the first day of Lent. We can all get together in a state of repentance. Jesus, according to Matthew's Gospel, said that we should wipe those ashes off our faces and keep our acts of penance to ourselves: "Whenever you fast, do not look dismal, like the hypocrites, for they disfigure their faces so as to show others that they are fasting" (Matt 6:16). But keeping those ashes on your face does not necessarily mean pulling a long face. Ashes on the forehead make every face a bit comic, like a clown's face daubed with spots. The ashes on my face and the ashes on yours speak to each other in a crowded subway car, in an office building corridor, on a wintry sidewalk: "Pardon my foolishness. I would like to start over again."

Ashes have the advantage over torn garments that they do less harm to your clothing. A certain ritual tearing of garments (e.g., the unstitching of a jacket shoulder seam) still characterizes the pious practice of Orthodox Jews in mourning. The prophet Joel, possibly writing in postexilic Judah, urges his readers to leave their stitches in when mourning their sins: "Rend your hearts and not your clothing. Return to the Lord, your God" (Joel 2:13). External signs of mourning mean very little unless we make an effort to let God break into the tiny fortress of the heart.

Saint Paul, writing to the unruly Christian community at Corinth, draws attention to the fact that repentance is not just a private or individual affair. Paul appealed to the strife-torn community to "be reconciled to God" (2 Cor 5:20). To be reconciled with the Creator draws in its wake reconciliation with our fellow creatures, our fellow sinners. If we label ourselves in a comic and public fashion as fools and sinners on Ash Wednesday, we have a good precedent in the one who was crucified on a charge of blasphemy: "For our sake [God] made him to be sin who knew no sin, so that in him we might become the righteousness of God" (2 Cor 5:21).

When Jesus claimed for himself the right to inaugurate the rule of God, his contemporaries accused him of blasphemy (Mark 14:64; John 8:59). Adam and Eve, in the story of Genesis, had succumbed to the temptation to such self-divinization (Gen 3:5). But Jesus was justified in claiming equality with God and we are not. Dying for the sin of Adam and Eve and for all human refusal to accept creatureliness, Jesus abolished our alienation from God and introduced us into his own holiness. In confronting our own mortality—ashes to ashes, dust to dust—we have cause for celebration. "When you fast, put oil on your head and wash your face" (Matt 6:17). The beginning of Lent is also the beginning of Easter. During Lent we might chew on that paradox for forty days instead of chewing on cigars, Twinkies and the ears of our long-suffering families.

THURSDAY AFTER ASH WEDNESDAY
Readings: Deuteronomy 30:15–20; Luke 9:22–25

The Thursday after Ash Wednesday, second of the four weekdays added to the six weeks of Lent to make for forty weekdays of penance (Lenten Sundays, like all Sundays, participate too much in the joy of Easter to admit of penance) is often the day on which our voluntary ambition to fast or to abstain from some pleasure (alcohol, tobacco, dessert, a good argument) falters. The Liturgy of the Word aims to encourage us to hang on to the decision we made on Ash Wednesday to join in the rigors of the Lord's uphill journey towards the cross.

Moses, delivering his final address in the Pentateuch, urges the people of Israel to remain faithful to the covenant they have struck with God at Sinai. The Book of Deuteronomy itself, a seventh-century B.C. revision of the more primitive expressions of covenantal law in Exodus, is really a series of exhortations to go beyond the externals of religious observance and penetrate to the core—the heart—of Israelite faith in Yahweh. "I have set before you today life and prosperity, death and adversity" (Deut 30:15). Life in this context does not merely consist in physical survival after death, but vibrant existence according to the covenant Yahweh struck with Israel. The opposite of such vibrant existence, being "led astray to bow down to other gods and serve them" (Deut 30:17), is a death more complete than the slavery Israel knew in Egypt. The gods we serve today—one or another addiction, consumerism, bigotry, selfishness—can enslave us more subtly than the animal-headed deities imaged in the ancient temples along the banks of the Nile. "Choose life so that you and your descendants may live" (Deut 30:19).

In the first prediction of his passion and death in the Gospel of Luke Jesus asks his disciples to make their choice for life as well, but life achieved in a most paradoxical fashion: by choosing the disgrace of public execution in following Jesus. "If any want to become my followers, let them deny themselves and take up their cross daily and follow me" (Luke 9:23). How could Jesus have used the image of taking up the cross as a daily duty for his followers before he himself made the cross the ultimate Christian symbol? Some have suggested that the cross of his original words may have referred to the paradoxical visionary passage in the prophecy of Ezekiel where the prophet glimpses an angelic scribe who is told to mark the foreheads of those who will survive the destruction of Jerusalem in 587 B.C. The scribe is to mark them with the last letter of the Hebrew alphabet, *taw*, which, in Hebrew before it adopted the Aramaic alphabet, was made like an X. Such forehead marking normally distinguished prisoners condemned to death from those only punished with imprisonment. In Ezekiel's vision, however, those so marked for destruction would actually survive: "Go through the city, through Jerusalem, and put a mark on the foreheads of those who sigh and groan over all the abominations that are committed in it....Touch no one who has the mark" (Ezek 9:4, 6). On Ash Wednesday we were marked with ashes in the form of a cross, daubed with the symbol of death so that we might learn how to live. "Those who want to save their life will lose it, and those who lose their life for my sake will save it" (Luke 9:24).

FRIDAY AFTER ASH WEDNESDAY
Readings: Isaiah 58:1–9; Matthew 9:14–15

Modern Muslims, looking for reasons other than repentance for sin to justify why they fast during the daylight hours of an entire lunar month every year, often offer the suggestion that fasting makes those who fast freely more aware of those who have to fast because they have so little to eat during all the months of the year, day and night. In offering this apologetic motif they are not far from the spirit of the third and last major author in the prophetic tradition of Isaiah, probably a citizen of Jerusalem in the priestly atmosphere of the fifth century B.C. fed up with the public asceticism of the officially pious. Third Isaiah speaks on God's behalf: "Look, you serve your own interest on your fast day, and oppress all your workers. Look, you fast only to quarrel and to fight....Will you call this a fast, a day acceptable to the Lord?" (Isa 58:3–4, 5). Yahweh goes on to enumerate through the prophet the central element involved in true fasting: refraining from oppression of the poor. For those who fast from injustice, "Your vindicator shall go before you, the glory of the Lord shall be your rear guard" (Isa 58:8). For those of us tempted to look on

Lent as a time to diet, Third Isaiah stops us in our tracks. Lent might be better spent in volunteering at a soup kitchen.

Jesus shocked his pious contemporaries, including the disciples of the ascetical John the Baptist, by not urging his followers to fast, a practice associated with mourning not only for the deceased but also for reversals in Israel's past. "The wedding guests cannot mourn as long as the bridegroom is with them, can they?" (Matt 9:15). They can, but they will spoil the wedding feast. Jesus, the bridegroom of a new Israel, proved to be very different not only from John the Baptist but also from the community for whom Matthew wrote his Gospel, a community that may have continued the Pharisaic tradition of fasting on Wednesdays and Fridays. Matthew ascribed to Jesus words inspired by the Holy Spirit: "The days will come when the bridegroom is taken away from them, and then they will fast" (Matt 9:15). Did Matthew and his community not realize that Jesus had risen from the dead and mourning for him was inappropriate? They did, but they knew that they themselves had still not entered into the wedding banquet of the end of time, and they fasted in preparation for it.

SATURDAY AFTER ASH WEDNESDAY
Readings: Isaiah 58:9–14; Luke 5:27–32

Despite all the hard things said about the Pharisees and their scribes or legal scholars in the New Testament, it sometimes seems that they have survived not only in the Orthodox tradition of Judaism but also in the membership of not a few Christian churches. Many Christian Pharisees and their spokespersons on legal matters are would-be canon lawyers. (Real canon lawyers usually know better.) Some Christian Pharisees set themselves up as critics of the church's mildness in dealing with repentant swindlers, the messily divorced and other Christians with less than a thick dossier of good deeds with which to make their way into heaven.

In dealing mildly with sinners whose misdeeds are documented in the popular press, the Christian churches have a good model in Jesus himself. The gospel reading for this fourth weekday preceding the first week of Lent presents Jesus shocking "the Pharisees and their scribes" (Luke 5:30) by calling to discipleship a member of a much-hated class of sinners in Roman Palestine, tax collectors. Tax collectors at that time were not so much ordinary operatives of a legitimate revenue service as they were agents of a hated colonial power (Rome) which distributed such appointments to Jewish quislings who gouged their fellow Jews for whatever they could extract for Rome and for themselves. Mark, Matthew and Luke all tell this story of Jesus recruiting a disciple from such a disreputable company. Called Levi by Mark and Luke, Matthew may be signing his Gospel by calling him Matthew (Matt 9:9).

Jesus defends himself in Luke's account not by justifying colonial tax gouging but by insisting on the medicinal nature of his ministry among "tax collectors and sinners" (Luke 5:30): "Those who are well have no need of a physician, but those who are sick" (Luke 5:31). Third Isaiah would have liked that approach to oppressors: as sick people rather than as the misunderstood rich. Continuing from yesterday with his social justice interpretation of fasting, the prophet lays out an agenda not only for repentant tax collectors but for all who would like to make a new start in their love for God and for humanity: "If you remove the yoke from among you, the pointing of the finger, the speaking of evil, if you offer your food to the hungry and satisfy the needs of the afflicted, then your light shall rise in the darkness and your gloom be like noonday" (Isa 58:9–10). The kinship between Third Isaiah and later Pharisee piety can be seen in the subsequent verses of the first reading, when he adds to his encomium for practitioners of social justice fulsome praise as well for those who scrupulously keep the Sabbath rest. If the Sabbath is seen in its original setting as provision for weekly rest for workers (see Exod 20:10), the instinct of Third Isaiah may not be that far removed from his exhortation to concern for the poor and the oppressed.

Chapter 2

THE FIRST WEEK
OF LENT

FIRST SUNDAY OF LENT (A)
Readings: Genesis 2:7–9, 3:1–7; Romans 5:12–19;
Matthew 4:1–11

GARDEN AND DESERT

The Middle East first experienced considerable desertifica-
tion about 6000 years ago, a process that hastened the development of systematic agriculture. Part of that development entailed
the enclosure of watered gardens or parks, walled paradises
where the ravages of desiccation and the foraging of hungry
flocks could be withstood. To the present day, the enclosed garden provides the aridity of the area between the Nile and the
Oxus with welcome relief. The readings for the first Sunday of
Lent move from the watered Garden of Eden to the desert of
Judea, providing in the process something of a panorama of the
history of sin and redemption.

In the familiar and often misunderstood narrative of the primal sin of humankind, the setting is the most perfect of gardens,
one laid out by God. The human being (in Hebrew, *'adam*)
formed out of clay (in Hebrew, *'adamah*) rejects such humble
origins (see Gen 2:7) and accedes to the suggestion that divine
honors are due him and his equal spouse as the primeval human
couple. "God knows that when you eat of it your eyes will be
opened, and you will be like God" (Gen 3:5), the tempter suggests, and the tempted listen with alacrity. The aboriginal parents

of humankind, the man and the woman, one in their human vocation to provide a partial image of a God otherwise unimaginable (Gen 1:27), mistake the imagery for the imaged. The serpent, "more crafty than any other wild animal" (Gen 3:1), persuades both man and woman that the God they image is plural, made after their own image.

Willfully deluded by the serpent, the man and the woman find themselves no longer at one with God nor at one with each other. "Then the eyes of both were opened, and they knew that they were naked" (Gen 3:7). They no longer saw the conjoined image of God in each other but only an embarrassing and solitary objectivity, a differentness that estranged them one from the other. The history of sin begins with a rejection of human limitations, with a craving for more than human power. The newly created human beings, fresh from the experience of their creation, want to be procreative father and mother divinities such as were typical of the religious traditions of so many of Israel's neighbors in the Middle East. In these religious traditions the mating of male and female divinities corresponded to the agricultural cycle and was deemed to affect it. Israelites settled in Canaan, no longer merely driving sheep and cattle but also engaged in agricultural pursuits, could be tempted to participate in such pragmatic forms of worship. Much of the history of Israel's compromises with the sexual sacramentalism of the fertility religion of Canaan may be alluded to in the story of our primeval parents in the Garden of Eden. The man and the woman, hungry for power and wealth and territoriality, ate. The garden they hoped to make their divine abode was blighted forever.

From the lush setting of Eden we move to the barren desert of Judea. Jesus fasted there for forty days and forty nights, in Matthew's account. Temptations came to him to exercise his power as Son of God on his own behalf: to assuage his hunger, to test God's loving concern for him, to exercise Solomonic royal power over the whole world. The gospel reading presents us with

Jesus, God and humanity at one, entering into his lifelong struggle with the Evil One, the spirit of grasping for power. The temptations provided by the devil in the desert sum up all the temptations Jesus experienced, and especially the temptations to messianic power arising from the promptings of his disciples (Matt 16:23) and the longings of the crowd (John 6:15).

In Matthew's Gospel the tempter is presented as unsure what the voice of God meant by the proclamation at the baptism of Jesus: "This is my Son, the beloved" (Matt 3:17). Was Jesus an adoptive Son of God, like the Davidic king at his enthronement (Ps 2:6–7)? Was Jesus the Son of God like Israel in the Exodus era (Hos 11:1)? The tempter probed, as the disciples and the crowd probed, but Jesus never made a false move. He did not feed himself or the multitude with the bread of political demagoguery. He did not overwhelm the Jerusalem skeptics by a feat demonstrating his intimacy with God. Finally, and most dramatically in Matthew's account of the temptations, he did not renounce his unique relationship with God simply to attain merely human domination over "all the kingdoms of the world and their splendor" (Matt 4:8). Jesus preferred the poverty of being merely human, refusing to disclose his full identity to the Evil One. In the desert of Judea he reversed the sin committed in the Garden of Eden. God's Son insisted on his frail humanity in order to counteract and overcome frail humanity's pretensions to divine status. Triumphant after this victory, Jesus accepted angelic homage.

Paul meditates in the second reading on the sin of "one man" (Rom 5:12) and the saving deed of "the one who was to come" (Rom 5:14). Jesus committed himself in the baptism he accepted from John to identification with sinners (see Matt 3:13–15). In the temptation in the desert he hid his more than human power. On the cross, finally, he lived out to the full the destiny of merely human beings, selflessly identified with sinners. It is from Paul that we derive our Christian notion that the sin of Adam affected all of us, turning us away from our createdness and leading us into the delusion of pseudodivinity. "Sin came into the world through one man, and death came through sin, and so death spread to all, because all have sinned" (Rom 5:12). But Paul was much more interested in the effective reversal of that primordial mistake by a new Adam. "If the many died through the one man's trespass, much more surely have the grace of God and the free gift in the grace of the one man, Jesus Christ, abounded for the many" (Rom 5:15).

A river of grace rises in the desert; a new Eden, populated by the progeny of the new Adam, lies in the future.

Candidates for baptism at Easter, accompanied by their sponsors, are formally presented to the worshiping community on this Sunday in the Rite of Election. Both godparents and candidates are asked to testify before the community as to the seriousness of their intention. The candidates then give their names for inscription in the list of those chosen to be baptized. The celebrant leads the congregation in praying for those so enrolled, asking God to count them among his adopted children, reborn into a new covenant. Not yet full members of the worshiping community, the elect are then asked to depart from the church before the Liturgy of the Eucharist commences. But even in this temporary banishment they can discern the gracious welcome that lies in the near future, when they will be baptized into the new Adam.

FIRST SUNDAY OF LENT (B)
Readings: Genesis 9:8–15; 1 Peter 3:18–22; Mark 1:12–15

ALONE IN A WASTELAND

The human person stands, in the biblical hierarchy of creatures, halfway between the beasts and the angels. Psalm 8 praises the Lord for making us "a little lower than God" and yet enabling us to rule over the other animals: "all sheep and oxen, and also the beasts of the field, the birds of the air, and the fish of the sea, and whatever passes along the paths of the seas" (Ps 8: 5, 7–8). Neither so spiritual as the angels nor so carnal as the animals, we sometimes feel lonely in our universe. The first Sunday of Lent gives us time to reflect on the uniquely human loneliness of enfleshed spirit or inspirited flesh.

Mark's account of the testing of Jesus in the desert, very different from the narratives of Matthew and Luke, tells us how Jesus, fresh from his experience at the Jordan of "the heavens torn apart and the Spirit descending like a dove on him" (Mark 1:10), felt driven by that same Spirit into the desert. The desert, at least in the ancient Near East, seemed to most observers the quintessential bastion of death, a place where vegetation (with rare exceptions) had died and where animals, and especially the human animal, found it difficult to survive. Spirits, on the other hand, found the desert almost a natural habitat, a place where they could thrive. For evil spirits, in particular, or those capricious sprites whom the Arabs call *jinn* (genies), the desert provided a congenial (the pun is intended!) setting.

Mark's brief account of the temptation in the desert stresses the serene victory of Jesus over the land of desolation and its erstwhile master, Satan. "He was in the wilderness forty days, tempted by Satan" (Mark 1:13). But Jesus triumphed over both wild animals and wilder spirits in this haunted environment, taming the wild animals and accepting the homage and service of the angels, the only spirits left in the desert after his forty days of combat there. "He was with the wild beasts; and the angels waited on him" (Mark 1:13).

The other readings point to this gospel theme. In his lonely rule over the desert and its denizens, Jesus bore a striking resemblance to the ruler of the creation restored after the flood, Noah. "I am establishing my covenant with you and your descendants after you, and with every living creature that is with you" (Gen 9:9–10). Thus God made Noah the master of what remained after the devastation of the flood. Both Noah and Jesus are presented to us on this first Sunday of Lent as survivors, those who have outlasted a long ordeal and who begin life again, chastened by the experience. After the desolation of the flood, God established with Noah and his family a covenant of peace. Through them God extended peace to "the birds, the domestic animals, and every animal of the earth with you, as many as came out of the ark" (Gen 9:10). The rainbow, God's bow laid down as a gesture of peacemaking, symbolizes the pact established through Noah, a lonely person who braved the floodwaters of sin that engulfed his generation.

The First Epistle of Peter picks up this image, suggesting the lonely uniqueness of Christ engaged in the work of our salvation, "the righteous for the unrighteous" (1 Pet 3:18). The ark that rescued Noah and his family suggests to the author of this epistle not "a removal of dirt from the body, but…an appeal to God for a good conscience" (1 Pet 3:21). Jesus, the lonely conqueror "with angels, authorities, and powers made subject to him" (1 Pet 3:22), rules after his triumph over all lesser powers. By an odd paradox, baptismal drowning in Jesus proves to be the ark that rescues us from the floodwaters of sin.

After a century of holocausts, we need to meditate on survivors. The First Epistle of Peter describes the death of Jesus and his survival, first of all, in the realm of the dead: "He went and made a proclamation to the spirits in prison" (1 Pet 3:19). By those spirits in prison the author means the nonsurvivors of the flood, who "in former times did not obey, when God waited patiently in the days of Noah" (1 Pet 3:20). But even those imprisoned spirits had the chance to hear the good news from Jesus triumphant over death, a thought that should give hope to those who worry about the fate of the unbaptized or those who, to our eyes, die unrepentant. All of us have the chance of survival through the waters of baptism, which Peter paradoxically sees as the symbolic parallel of Noah's ark. All of this is made possible by the empowering survival of Jesus, who "has gone into heaven and is at the right hand of God" (1 Pet 3:22). So enthroned above every form of life, Jesus offers us the possibility of new life through repentance and faith in him.

Like Noah and Jesus, we are destined for testing by the contending forces in the midst of which we live. At the beginning of this season of repentance and reevaluation, we accept the loneliness of being human, of being tested.

FIRST SUNDAY OF LENT (C)
Readings: Deuteronomy 26:4–10; Romans 10:8–13;
Luke 4:1–13

PROFESSING FAITH

The earliest baptismal practice of the church involved a threefold profession of faith in God as Father, Son and Spirit combined with threefold plunging of the catechumen into the waters of rebirth. These sacramental actions crowned a long series of testings and rites of initiation. The season of Lent, which makes its formal debut this Sunday after four weekdays of preview, originally aimed at preparing prospective Christians for their baptism. This Sunday's Liturgy of the Word centers on the profession of faith that baptism entails.

In the first reading, excerpted from the Deuteronomist's description of the ceremonial offering of first fruits, the descendant of Jacob-Israel, "a wandering Aramean...[who] went down into Egypt and lived there as an alien" (Deut 26:5), gives the first fruits of the Promised Land in praise of the Lord. Israelite faith centered on the wonder of Exodus, the marvelous way in which Yahweh rescued oppressed nomads, gave them a national identity as Israel, and settled them in the country of the Canaanites. Reliance on God rather than on human means lies at the center of Israelite faith, as the credal statement at the offering of the first fruits insists. In every trial, the descendants of Jacob-Israel had to cry out to "the Lord, the God of our ancestors" (Deut 26:7) and the Lord came to their rescue "with a mighty hand and an outstretched arm, with a terrifying display of power, and with signs and wonders" (Deut 26:8).

The second reading, taken from Paul's treatment of Israelite chosenness in his letter to the Jewish-Christian community in Rome, deals with the quintessential Christian profession of faith: "Jesus is Lord" (Rom 10:9). Precisely as Lord, Yahweh who rescued Israel from Egypt, Jesus broke through the limitations of particularity and offered deliverance from the bondage of sin to all humankind. "There is no distinction between Jew and Greek; the same Lord is Lord of all and is generous to all who call on him" (Rom 10:12). Paul asserts that all of us, like Jacob-Israel and Jesus, must put our faith in God: "For one believes with the heart and so is justified, and one confesses with the mouth and so is saved" (Rom 10:10).

An eleventh-century geographer writing in Muslim Spain, al-Bakri, described the matrilineal succession of sororal nephew to maternal uncle in the court of ancient Ghana (in present-day Mauritania and Mali), a practice the patrilineal Muslim writer found very strange. "This is their custom and their habit," he wrote, "that the kingship is inherited by the son of the king's sister. He has no doubt that his successor is a son of his sister, while he is not certain that his son is in fact his own, and he is not convinced of his relationship to him." Something of the same suspicion of an heir's legitimacy infected the imagination of the adversary of humankind, the devil, according to the Gospel of Luke. At his baptism Jesus had been acclaimed as God's "Son, the Beloved" (Luke 3:22), and Luke traced his sonship through Joseph (Luke 3:23) back through David and Abraham and Adam to God (Luke 3:24–38). But the devil was not sure what all this meant. Throughout the life of Jesus, as in the life of any child of

God, the adversary kept probing to find out if there were any weaknesses in the truth.

The first and third interrogations of Jesus by the prosecuting attorney in the desert began with a crucial conditional clause: "If you are the Son of God..." (Luke 4:3, 9). The second interrogation in Luke (the third in Matthew) skips the conditional clause, content to reduce sonship to God to worldly messiahship, imperial rule like that of Solomon: "Then the devil led him up and showed him in an instant all the kingdoms of the world" (Luke 4:5). Jesus, like a well-rehearsed client of a clever lawyer, never quite answered the devil's questions, relying instead on the Book of Deuteronomy. John's Gospel attributed lawyerly characteristics to the Holy Spirit, the Paraclete (John 16:7–11). Luke simply asserts that Jesus entered into this desert trial "full of the Holy Spirit" and "led by the Spirit" (Luke 4:1).

The adversary tested Jesus on his sonship to Adam and his sonship to God. The newly baptized Jesus proved true to his human and divine ancestries. From the faithless adversary Jesus concealed his divinity, his oneness with God, and emphasized his humanity, his oneness with us. But implicit in his answers to the adversary's probing can be found, with the eyes of faith, an assertion of his divinity: "Worship the Lord, your God, and serve only him" (Luke 4:8, citing Deut 6:13). This portrait of Jesus professing his faith—in the desert, overlooking the kingdoms of the world, poised on the parapet of the Temple—arrests our attention at the beginning of Lent. Jesus proved himself both a faithful God and a faithful descendant of Adam. "No one who believes in him will be put to shame," Paul declares, paraphrasing Isaiah (Rom 10:11, citing Isa 28:16). Our humanity will also be tempted, probed by the adversary. But putting our faith in the God who embraced our humanity to its core, we can look forward to ultimate victory over evil in him.

MONDAY OF THE FIRST WEEK OF LENT
Readings: Leviticus 19:1–2, 11–18; Matthew 25:31–46

Many modern secularists are willing to grant that the so-called second tablet of the Law of Moses, the fourth through the tenth commandments in the catechetical count most familiar to Catholics, sums up a basic ethical code, give or take a few details, with which most human beings want to live. Obedience to parental and other forms of legitimate authority, abstention from murderous violence, refraining from adultery, theft, fraud and the covetousness that leads to such crimes: common sense demands that we live like that. Civil law, however, seldom enters into such internal matters as the various forms of covetousness. But secularists feel greater discomfort with the less utilitarian "first tablet": the commandments centered on Israel's relationship to God.

The Book of Leviticus, a work originating in priestly circles and written down at some time like the Babylonian exile when the levitical priests had less to occupy them than they might normally have had when the Temple was functioning in Jerusalem, makes very uncomfortable reading for secularists. It combines the two tablets of the Law as the two eyes of any human being combine what they see into one. "You shall be holy," God tells the people of Israel, "for I the Lord your God am holy" (Lev 19:2). What does holiness mean in this context? Something quite other than morality: the holiness of Yahweh consists in the differentness of God, the irreducibility of the divine Reality to anything else. Yahweh was very different from the fertility gods and goddesses of Israel's neighbors. Not so much interested in ritual sacrifice (despite the earlier chapters of Leviticus), Yahweh demanded of the people of Israel that they too be different from their neighbors, not for any practical reasons of commonsense morality, but precisely because they were the people of a very different God. "You shall not be partial to the poor nor defer to the great: with justice you shall judge your neighbor....I am the Lord" (Lev 19:15, 16). In other words, the people of Israel were to imitate the differentness of God.

It is easier, then, to see why Jesus could join together as one commandment (Mark 12:29–32; Matt 22:37–39; Luke 10:27–28) a divine directive from Deuteronomy ("You shall love the Lord your God with all your heart, and with all your soul, and with all your might" [Deut 6:5]) with a command from this particular passage in Leviticus ("You shall love your neighbor as yourself" [Lev 19:18]). The very point of this section of the Holiness Code in the Book of Leviticus is that we must profess in the concrete our love for the God we cannot see by loving our neighbors whom we can see but would prefer to overlook. The gospel passage for this first Monday of Lent spells this out in Matthew's account of the final judgment. Humankind is judged for its recognition of the presence of Jesus, the fullness of God expressed in human terms, in the hungry, the thirsty, the stranger, the naked, the sick, the imprisoned. We recognize the holiness and differentness of God and of Jesus when we reach out to God and to Jesus in the abandoned of this world. "Truly, I tell you, just as you did it to one of the least of these who are members of my family, you did it to me" (Matt 25:40).

TUESDAY OF THE FIRST WEEK OF LENT
Readings: Isaiah 55:10–11; Matthew 6:7–15

One of the finest films made in the 1960s, Arthur Penn's *The Miracle Worker*, portrays Annie Sullivan gradually teaching Helen Keller, blind and deaf from very early childhood, how to speak. From Keller's memory of water and its connection with the infant sound *wa-wa*, Sullivan was able to develop in this extraordinary woman an ability to express herself, freeing her from the bonds of silence.

The scriptures of both the Old Testament and the New teach us that God, not entirely unlike Annie Sullivan, first elicited from us the words with which we can address the otherwise almost unapproachable divine majesty. At the conclusion of the written work ascribed to Second Isaiah, the gifted poet and prophet of the return of the Jews from the Babylonian exile in the late sixth century B.C., the prophet reminds us, on God's behalf, that God's word must come to us from God before we can utter it ourselves. "For as the rain and the snow come down from heaven and do not return there until they have watered the earth, making it bring forth and sprout, giving seed to the sower and bread to the eater, so shall my word be that goes out from my mouth" (Isa 55:10–11). The prophetic word is referred to in this passage, of course, but the same thing applies as well to the word of prayer. Saint Paul, in the Epistle to the Romans, insists that "the Spirit helps us in our weakness; for we do not know how to pray as we ought, but that very Spirit intercedes with sighs too deep for words" (Rom 8:26).

Jesus came to the aid of his disciples when he taught them how to pray, noting in the process that they should avoid the temptation to "heap up empty phrases as the Gentiles do" (Matt 6:7), by which he presumably meant the rhetorically windy denizens of the Greek- and Latin-speaking world of the first century A.D. Not every officially composed ecclesiastical prayer of later centuries has heeded this advice. Jesus assured his contemporaries, and he continues to assure us, that "your Father knows what you need before you ask him" (Matt 6:8). Nevertheless, for our own sake, if not for God's, we need to learn how to pray. Liturgical and private usage over twenty centuries has taught us to recite Matthew's version of the Lord's Prayer, rather than Luke's (Luke 11:2–4). Neither was meant so much to be repeated as a formulary as to be used as a model. The basic point of what Jesus taught us to do when we pray is (a) to leave everything to God, but (b), within that context of self-surrender, to ask for what we need. Thus the first part of the Our Father repeats in three different ways ("Hallowed be your name. Your kingdom come. Your will be done" [Matt 6:9–10]) what Jesus finally prayed for in the Garden of Gethsemane: "Yet not what I want but what you want...your will be done" (Matt 26:39, 42). The second part of the Our Father, however, asks for specific needs (daily sustenance, forgiveness of debts, deliverance from the final trial) as did Jesus in Gethsemane ("Let this cup pass from me" [Matt 26:39]), but always with the proviso that God's will comes first.

In terms of our own feelings, we may not always be happy with praying that God's will, not ours, be done. But this is the word that has come down to us from God when the ineffable Mystery broke out of the eternal silence and spoke our human language. Jesus was not spared the cup of suffering, and we may not be spared it either, but Jesus has taught us how to pray above all else that God's will be done.

WEDNESDAY OF THE FIRST WEEK OF LENT
Readings: Jonah 3:1–10; Luke 11:29–32

If there were to be a contest to choose a biblical patron saint for cranks, the prophet Jonah would surely win the prize. The author of this exceptional prophetic work probably intended the figure of Jonah, whose name means "dove" in Hebrew, to symbolize God's people either in exile or surviving in the larger world that opened up for Israel with the collapse of the Northern Kingdom under Assyrian assault (721 B.C.) and the Southern Kingdom with the Babylonian exile (587 B.C.). In God's mysterious providence, these experiences of disaster opened up both Israel and Judah to the possibility of Gentiles, even such hated people as the Ninevites, coming to know the Lord.

Thus the prophet Jonah was sent by the Lord not to preach to his fellow Jews but to the denizens of the Assyrian capital,

Nineveh. Attempting to escape this unenviable vocation, Jonah headed by sea in the opposite direction, landing up not in Tarshish (thought by some scholars to be Spain) but in the belly of a great fish when he was thrown overboard to placate the Lord who had stirred up a storm to punish his delinquent prophet (chapter 1). Surviving this ordeal, Jonah turned in repentance to the Lord, who delivered him in one piece from his aquatic prison (chapter 2). Taking up, once again, his mission to the hated Ninevites, Jonah discovered that even they were capable of repentance, something he petulantly regretted (chapter 4). Suitably enough for the second Wednesday of the Lenten season, Jonah reminds us that the time of repentance left to us neo-Ninevites is short: "Forty days more and Nineveh shall be overthrown" (Jonah 3:4). We are called to join not only the citizens of Nineveh but also their ascetic cattle and sheep in fasting: "No human being or animal, no herd or flock, shall taste anything" (Jonah 3:7).

Jesus, less concerned with the externals of fasting, saw in Jonah a sign of the extension of chosenness beyond the borders of Israel. "Just as Jonah became a sign to the people of Nineveh, so the Son of Man will be to this generation" (Luke 11:30). His contemporaries in Israel demanded of Jesus more and more miraculous deeds, without responding to those deeds in faith. Tragedy loomed on the horizon for those who neglected the signs of God's power to save. The sign of Jonah, in this particular passage of Luke's Gospel, consists in the response of the Gentile Ninevites, traditional enemies of Israel, to Jonah proclaiming the prophetic word of God. The sign of the Queen of Sheba (1 Kgs 10:1–10) has a similar significance: "She came from the ends of the earth to listen to the wisdom of Solomon, and see, something greater than Solomon is here!" (Luke 11:31). If the Chosen People do not respond to the prophetic word and royal wisdom of God in faith, others will replace them. And if we Christians of the North Atlantic world do not respond to the word and wisdom of God in Christ in our generation, others may replace us as well.

THURSDAY OF THE FIRST WEEK OF LENT
Readings: Esther C:12, 14–16, 23–25 [=Esth 14:1, 3–5, 12–14 NRSV]; Matthew 7:7–12

Jews celebrate annually the feast of Purim ("lots") sometime in February or March, depending on the correspondence of the civil calendar with 14–15 Adar in the Jewish calendar. The "lots" in the naming of the feast refer to the changes wrought by God's providence in the lot of those diaspora Jews who continued to live in the Persian Empire after the time of the Babylonian exile and the return of other Jews to Jerusalem. The story of this Persian pogrom, one of the many that have marked Jewish history, ends in the Book of Esther with a happy reversal of fortune.

Haman, said to be the vizier of the Persian emperor Ahasuerus or Xerxes (r. 485–464 B.C.), plays the part of the villain in this story. This Persian anti-Semite, the fictional prototype of all those who have wanted to slaughter Jews for their differentness, found himself instead led to the gallows. The eponymous heroine of the story, Esther (Hadassah in Hebrew), is a devout but discreet Jewish woman, a member of the harem of Ahasuerus promoted to the place of chief wife when another wife defaulted in her duties as official hostess. She managed to turn Ahasuerus against Haman and saved Israel in exile from another potential disaster. The first reading for this Lenten weekday features a prayer of Esther (found in the Greek, but not the surviving Hebrew text), a model of fervent petition. As in much of Jewish prayer, the memory of God's past benefactions to Israel is summoned up before the petitioner gets to the point: "You, O Lord, took Israel out of all the nations, and our ancestors from among all their forbears, for an everlasting inheritance" (Esth C:16 [Esth 14:5]). Then comes the eloquent petition for rhetorical power to turn Ahasuerus against Haman and to reverse the dreaded lot of the Jews: "Put eloquent speech in my mouth before the lion, and turn his heart to hate the man who is fighting against us" (Esth C:24 [Esth 14:13]).

Jesus, who in Tuesday's excerpt from Matthew taught us how to pray, comes back to the theme in today's gospel, also taken from Matthew's Sermon on the Mount. "Ask, and it will be given to you; search, and you will find; knock, and the door will be opened for you" (Matt 7:7). Those who have often asked and searched and knocked at heaven's gate may want to question the ease with which Jesus assures his disciples that their prayers of petition will always be answered. Many of us feel that we have all too often received stones when we asked for bread, or snakes when we asked for fish. But perhaps we have not prayed as Jesus taught us in the gospel two days ago: "Hallowed be your name. Your kingdom come. Your will be done" (Matt 6:9–10). Jesus assured his listeners and he continues to assure us that God the Father is even more generous than a human father: "If you then, who are evil, know how to give good gifts to your children, how much more will your Father in heaven give good things to those who ask him!" (Matt 7:11). The parallel verse in Luke makes more theologically specific what Jesus intended by the "good things" to be received by prayerful petition according to Matthew's text. "If you then, who are evil, know how to give good gifts to your children, how much more will the heavenly Father give the Holy Spirit to those who ask him!" (Luke 11:13). If we pray that God's will be done, our specific needs may not be granted, but we will receive, in answer to our prayer, the Gift of God: the outpouring of the divine Selfhood that we call the Holy Spirit.

FRIDAY OF THE FIRST WEEK OF LENT
Readings: Ezekiel 18:21–28; Matthew 5:20–26

Proverbs are not always intelligible on first hearing. It took me years to figure out what "You can't have your cake and eat it too" meant. How could one possibly eat a cake one didn't have? Eventually I came to realize that *have* in this sentence means "keep." Both the prophets Jeremiah (31:29) and Ezekiel (18:2) quote slight variations of a proverb current in Israel for many centuries: "The parents have eaten sour grapes, and the children's teeth are set on edge." The original intent of the proverb, hard for modern people to grasp, was that the iniquities committed by past generations exercise a baleful influence on their descendants as well. Such a notion of collective and inherited guilt arose in the context of Israel's national solidarity as a covenanted people: "I the Lord your God am a jealous God, punishing children for the iniquity of parents, to the third and the fourth generation of those who reject me, but showing steadfast love to the thousandth generation of those who love me and keep my commandments" (Exod 20:5–6). It is comforting, at least, to see that good deeds have a more lasting effect than evil ones, although the history of age-old hatreds in places like Rwanda and Burundi, the Balkans and Northern Ireland remind us of the realism of the first assertion.

The first reading comes from a celebrated chapter in the writings of the prophet of the Babylonian exile, Ezekiel. Speaking to Israelites no longer in the land of promise, the prophet urged them with God's words to take on the covenant as a personal rather than a merely communal morality. Thus, if sinners repent for previous bad behavior, neither they nor their descendants will suffer for it: "None of the transgressions that they have committed shall be remembered against them; for the righteousness that they have done they shall live" (Ezek 18:22). Likewise, if good people go bad, "none of the righteous deeds

31

that they have done shall be remembered; for the treachery of which they are guilty and the sin they have committed, they shall die" (Ezek 18:24). It doesn't matter what your ancestors did, bad or good; the principle of personal moral culpability here receives one of its first clear expressions.

In the gospel reading, excerpted from the Sermon on the Mount in Matthew like so many others in the first week and a half of Lent, Jesus urges an even greater personalization of moral culpability than did Ezekiel, bidding his disciples to go beneath the externals of sin and root out the interior dispositions that lead to sin. The fifth commandment forbids murder; Jesus condemns the hatred that lies behind it: "But I say to you that if you are angry with a brother or sister, you will be liable to judgment; and if you insult a brother or sister, you will be liable to the council; and if you say, 'You fool,' you will be liable to the hell of fire" (Matt 5:22). Literalists can trivialize this passage, unnecessarily causing scruples in people who occasionally lose their temper. Jesus is talking about an anger with deeper roots: the sort of hatred that spawned the Nazi holocaust of the Jews, Pol Pot's extermination of his fellow Cambodians, efforts at ethnic cleansing in the Great Lakes area of central Africa and the Balkans. There can probably never be an effective law against such radical hatred, but God's law, specified by Jesus himself, condemns the roots of murderousness in the human heart.

SATURDAY OF THE FIRST WEEK OF LENT
Readings: Deuteronomy 26:16–19; Matthew 5:43–48

Valedictory addresses often degenerate into the maudlin, but the most famous valedictory addresses in the Bible, the final sermons attributed to Moses in the Book of Deuteronomy and the last discourse of Jesus in the Gospel of John, prove to be among the most eloquent and moving passages in the scriptures. The liturgy for this final day of the first full week of Lent counterbalances a brief segment from the final words of Moses with the conclusion of the first part of the programmatic discourse of Jesus in the Gospel of Matthew, the Sermon on the Mount.

Secular covenants in the ancient Middle East, treaties between individuals or kingdoms, either as equal partners or as sovereigns and vassals, often included in their formulation some summary expression of the relationship agreed upon between the parties involved. The Hebrew Bible gives an example of a covenant between equals in the oath of friendship sworn between David and Jonathan: "The Lord shall be between me and you, and between my descendants and your descendants, forever" (1 Sam 20:42). The first reading shows how a covenant between unequals, e.g., God as Sovereign and Israel as God's vassal, was expressed. "Today you have obtained the Lord's agreement: to be your God; and for you to walk in his ways, to keep his statutes, his commandments, and his ordinances, and to obey him. Today the Lord has obtained your agreement: to be his treasured people, as he promised you, and to keep his commandments" (Deut 26:17–18). Abiding by the stipulations of such a covenant—God's fidelity to his choice of Israel and Israel's keeping of God's commandments—demonstrated the concreteness of that covenant in the lives of its vowed partners.

Jesus offered a deepening of the covenant originally struck with Israel at Sinai, demanding not only the externals of the commandments but even a change of heart. The people of Israel had been instructed by God to "love your neighbor as yourself" (Lev 19:18). But some took this to mean that they should conversely hate the people they defined as non-neighbors, the Gentile populations that surrounded them (see Deut 7:1–2). Jesus demanded the end of such narrowness. But note the realism of the command: the follower of Jesus is not asked to deny that some people may be enemies. "Love your enemies, and pray for those who persecute you" (Matt 5:44). Like the early civil rights demonstrators who followed the nonviolent leadership of Martin Luther King, Jr., the disciples of Jesus are to tell those beating them with truncheons or carting them off to jail, "I love you." The mention of Martin Luther King, Jr., and his model in such nonviolence, the Mahatma Gandhi, reminds us that such behavior sometimes can produce positive political effects. Even if it does not prove politically useful, however, it conforms us to God who loves even those who hate him: "He makes his sun rise on the evil and on the good, and sends rain on the righteous and on the unrighteous" (Matt 5:45). Imitating the absolute liberality of God, we can come closer and closer to the perfection of God's compassion: "Be perfect, therefore, as your heavenly Father is perfect" (Matt 5:48).

Chapter 3

THE SECOND WEEK
OF LENT

SECOND SUNDAY OF LENT (A)
Readings: Genesis 12:1–4; 2 Timothy 1:8–10; Matthew 17:1–9

TRIALS AND BLESSINGS

Saint Patrick, a Breton or Briton by birth, was enslaved by Irish pirates in the early fifth century and taken to their homeland to tend sheep. After six years' captivity he managed to escape his masters and return to his homeland. A nominal Christian until his enslavement, Patrick came to deeper faith in that time of adversity in a pagan environment. Years later, Patrick dreamed of Ireland and in his dreaming heard "the voice of the Irish" calling out to him: "I heard the voice of those who lived beside the wood of Voclut, which is near the Western sea. And thus they cried out: 'We ask you, boy, to come and walk among us once more.'" In the *Confession* in which he narrated this call experience, Patrick recognized the validity of his vocation: "Thanks be to God that after many years the Lord dealt with them according to their cry." Twenty years after his escape from Ireland, Patrick returned as a missionary bishop.

The voice of the Lord resounds throughout the readings for this second Sunday of Lent. In the first Genesis narrative of the call of Abraham (Abram), Yahweh subjected the patriarch to a terrible trial: exile "from your country and your kindred and your father's house" (Gen 12:1). In return for this trial, however, a sevenfold divine blessing was assured. Abraham himself became the quintessential model of the blessed person, the standard against which the blessings of others could be measured. Like Saint Patrick, however, Abraham experienced heartbreak first.

The writer in the school of Paul from whom the Second Epistle to Timothy derives addressed his exhortations to a Christian community experiencing external persecution and internal dissension, especially in the area of sound doctrine. Just as Paul had suffered in his generation in dealing with fractious communities like the Corinthians, Timothy, and later generations of community founders, were urged to "join with me in suffering for the gospel" (2 Tim 1:8). Blessings will follow trials, and we have only to submit to the "grace...given to us in Christ Jesus before the ages began" (2 Tim 1:9).

Matthew's account of the transfiguration reads like unmitigated blessing until we put it in its context. Just six days before the experience of Peter, James and John on a high mountain, Jesus had enunciated hard truths about the demands of discipleship. "If any want to become my followers, let them deny themselves and take up their cross and follow me" (Matt 16:24). But this doleful announcement was accompanied by a promise that "there are some standing here who will not taste death before they see the Son of Man coming in his kingdom" (Matt 16:28).

In some sense the transfiguration of Jesus fulfilled this promise. Peter, James and John glimpsed for a brief moment something of the resurrected glory that would come to Jesus after his crucifixion and death. The description of the transfigured Jesus by Matthew bears some resemblance to the portrait of the exalted Lord in the opening vision of the Book of Revelation: "I saw one like the Son of Man, clothed with a long robe and with a golden sash across his chest. His head and his hair were white as white wool, white as snow; his eyes were like a flame of fire" (Rev 1:13–14). The angel of the Lord in Matthew's account of the resurrection appears in similar splendor: "His appearance was like lightning, and his clothing white as snow" (Matt 28:3).

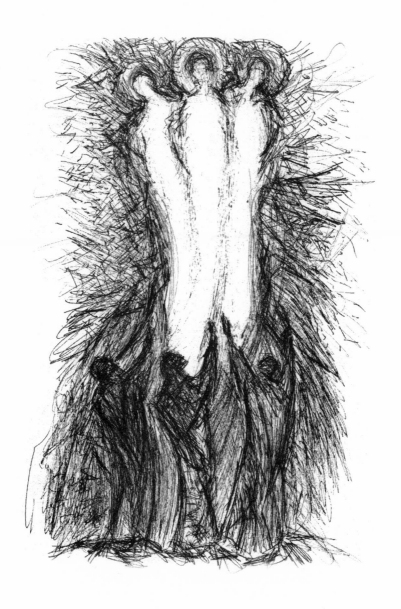

Moses and Elijah, the fountainheads of law and prophecy in the Israelite tradition, appeared with Jesus in glory. But when Peter, the principal visionary, mistakenly expressed the desire to equate Jesus with Moses and Elijah by building three booths to shelter these men of suffering now exalted, God intervened. "While he was still speaking, suddenly a bright cloud overshadowed them" (Matt 17:5). The presence of God (*shekhina*) that had filled the Temple, invisibly enthroned above the Ark of the Covenant, was often symbolized in the Hebrew Bible by a cloud refulgent with light. The divine presence in this vision abolished Moses and Elijah, law and prophecy, centering all of divine power on Jesus. "From the cloud a voice said, 'This is my Son, the beloved; with him I am well pleased; listen to him!'" (Matt 17:5).

Terror overwhelmed the disciples; the divine self-disclosure could kill a human being unprotected in God's presence. Jesus stood between them and God, reducing transcendent glory to tangible dimensions. "Jesus came and touched them, saying, 'Get up and do not be afraid'" (Matt 17:7). Only Matthew's account of the transfiguration mentions this touch of Jesus, a pungently human detail.

On the second Sunday of Lent the church always presents us with the mystery of the transfiguration, a foretaste of the blessings that will come after a lifetime of trial. In Lent we live out a time of trial interspersed with hints of the glory that is to come. Unlike the disciples who ascended that mountain with Jesus, we no longer have to maintain our silence about the vision bequeathed by God. In the Second Epistle attributed to Peter, the mature disciple become an apostle declares that "we had been eyewitnesses of his majesty...while we were with him on the holy mountain" (2 Pet 1:16, 18). With Peter we build not booths to shelter passing glory but a church through which God's glory might be seen throughout the world.

SECOND SUNDAY OF LENT (B)
*Readings: Genesis 22:1–2, 9, 10–13, 15–18; Romans 8:31–34;
Mark 9:2–10*

THE CRUCIAL DIFFERENCE

There are times in history when we feel, perhaps too romantically, that one person made the crucial difference between disaster and victory. Charles de Gaulle, at the liberation of Paris, strode through pouring rain into the Cathedral of Notre Dame to thank God for the deliverance of France. Even as he approached the cathedral, snipers were firing from rooftops at that towering figure so easy to single out in a crowd. Inside the cathedral, when an aide's pistol accidentally and harmlessly discharged, the terror-stricken companions of de Gaulle fell to the ground. Only de Gaulle remained standing. The French remembered that sort of courage more than a decade later in the shambles of the Fourth Republic, and invited de Gaulle to return to public life and rescue France from chaos and possible civil war.

The disciples of Jesus had heroized Jesus as their messiah in much the same way. When, in the passage immediately preceding this Sunday's gospel, Jesus revealed to them that his idea of messiahship involved suffering, rejection and death (Mark 8:31–9:1), not only for the messiah, but also for his followers, the disciples were naturally disheartened. In Mark's transfiguration story much emphasis is laid on Peter, James and John, the most politically ambitious disciples. In their puzzlement and frustration with Jesus and his renunciation of glorious messiahship in the manner of David and Solomon, they came face to face with the meaning of the cross: God's glory shining most brightly through one who was willing to surrender all ambition and die an outlaw's death. As in John's Gospel, such glorification combines the mysteries of Good Friday, Easter Sunday and Ascension Thursday.

Jesus stood out between Elijah and Moses as one whose death would be bloody and disgraceful. No chariot of fire for him like the one that came for Elijah (2 Kgs 2:11), no mysterious burial like that of Moses, perhaps by angels (Deut 34:5–6; Jude 9). And yet, paradoxically, the death of Jesus was to be glorious. Peter, true to form, missed the point of the transfiguration vision and wished to make this foretaste of glory a permanent event, a lasting Festival of Booths. But the *shekhina*, the mysterious presence of God, tabernacled on Jesus that day on the mountain, designating him as the only one destined to live and to die and to rise again as God's beloved Son in a unique sense. In Mark's Gospel Jesus is acclaimed as God's Son at his baptism by John, the transfiguration and the crucifixion, twice by God and once by a Roman centurion (Mark 15:39). The Gentile centurion is presented by Mark as understanding in the crucifixion what Peter, James and John could hardly comprehend in the glory of the transfiguration.

The first reading juxtaposes with the transfiguration another scene enacted on a mountaintop: the sacrifice of Isaac. Abraham had put all his hopes for the future on the child of promise, the only son he had with Sarah. Here too, God's way proved to be different from yours or mine. God seemed to demand the unimaginable from Abraham, a sacrifice all but consummated when the Lord's messenger intervened and substituted a ram as a holocaust in place of Isaac. Long before Calvary and the mountain of the transfiguration, God's glory shone through this wrenching trial of faith. "By your offspring," God told Abraham, "shall all the nations of the earth gain blessing for themselves, because you have obeyed my voice" (Gen 22:18). The children of Abraham, Isaac and Jacob have had to live out the mystery of near extinction in more than one succeeding generation. God continues to test his people's faith.

His obedience tested and proved, Abraham escaped the necessity of sacrificing his son in the long run. But God, who

made that terrible demand of Abraham and then rescinded it, finally made the same demand of himself and did not rescind it. Like Isaac, Jesus had more than an inkling of what was to come. In the passage just before this Sunday's gospel Jesus predicted his coming passion and death: "He began to teach them that the Son of Man must undergo great suffering, and be rejected by the elders, the chief priests, and the scribes, and be killed, and after three days rise again" (Mark 8:31).

In the second reading, Paul assures the Romans that God, "who did not withhold his own Son, but gave him up for all of us" (Rom 8:32), will eventually grant us the glory that we seek as well. But that glory will not come easily, rescuing us from a painful or a lonely death not unlike those of Elijah and Moses. For us who are marked from our baptism with the sign of the cross, glory only radiates through pain. Our leader on the path to glory, Jesus, made the crucial difference, turning the defeat of the crucifixion into a means of glorifying God. But the glorified and risen Jesus bore in his hands, feet and side the mark of the nails and the spear that pierced him. The glorious messiahship of Jesus, achieved only in his rising from the dead, never obliterated his identity as "the one whom they have pierced" (John 19:37, citing Zech 12:10). Even in his resurrection he bore the mark of the nails and the wound in his side (John 20:20, 27).

Martin Luther King, Jr., in a justly famous sermon, said that he had "been to the mountaintop" like Moses at the end of his life and had seen the Promised Land of freedom from its crest. When Dr. King was assassinated at the age of 39, these words were remembered. Had King lived as long as Charles de Gaulle, he might have made a crucial difference in how Americans reacted to the moral problems of later decades. Or he might have run for political office and forfeited much of the charism he exercised as a preacher. Paradoxically, his death assured him a more lasting glory than that of any of his surviving contemporaries in the civil rights movement.

In the aftermath of a century appalled by its history of genocide, torture and countless other forms of inhumanity, the cross bathed in glory makes the only sense that can be made of human iniquity. Just to survive we need to climb the mountain with Peter, James and John and catch a glimpse of God-irradiated flesh.

SECOND SUNDAY OF LENT (C)
Readings: Genesis 15:5–12, 17–18; Philippians 3:17–4:1; Luke 9:28–36

PATTERNED ON GLORY

The roofs of apartment houses in the major American cities with identifiable Jewish neighborhoods still sprout with temporary shelters made of branches and decorated with flowers every late September or early October. Although many Jews enjoy the autumn harvest festival, usually known as the Feast of Booths or Tabernacles *(Sukkoth)*, accounts vary as to why they build these fragile structures. One tradition historicizes the festival and asserts that the booths represent the temporary shelters in which the people of Israel sojourned in the desert during the years of the Exodus. Another tradition, more frankly agricultural, claims that the booths merely recall the shelters in which Israelite peasants in ancient times sought relief from the midday sun during the harvest season. Whatever their origin, the temporary nature of the booths seems to be central to their symbolic significance. The Feast of Booths, beginning five days after the Day of Atonement, contrasts strikingly with that mournful day of awe. Merriment characterizes the picnics in the booths just as sorrow for sin dominates Yom Kippur.

The Sundays of Lent, and particularly this second Sunday, participate to a certain degree in the tradition of following mournful sorrow with festive joy. Those who give up various pleasures during Lent will be happy to know that the six Sundays of this liturgical period do not count in the computation of the season's forty days of penitence and fasting. Like the three disciples whom Jesus took up a mountain to pray eight days after he had challenged them to deny themselves, take up their crosses daily and follow him (Luke 9:23), we look for some celebratory respite from the rigors of the first week of Lent.

But the respite is very temporary indeed. Even in glory Jesus spoke with Moses and Elijah, not about their triumphs over Pharaoh and Ahab, but about "his departure, which he was about to accomplish at Jerusalem" (Luke 9:31). More literally, that departure was in Luke's Greek the *exodos* of Jesus. For Moses, the Exodus from Egypt had brought very little personal satisfaction and much pain, culminating in his own inability to reach the Promised Land. "Although you may view the land from a distance, but you shall not enter it—the land that I am giving to the Israelites" (Deut 32:52). For Elijah, a life of prophetic suffering and unceasing movement finally ended with an exodus even more mysterious than that of Moses. Caught up in a chariot of fire (2 Kgs 2:11), Elijah departed this world of pain only to be met with the later Jewish expectation that he would return "before the great and terrible day of the Lord comes" (Mal 4: 5). Surely one lifetime of prophetic anxiety was enough!

Peter misunderstood the meaning of what he was seeing on the mountain; he wanted to make permanent what had to be temporary. Peter also equated Jesus with Moses and Elijah, but God cleared up this misunderstanding. As Moses and Elijah disappeared into the darkness of God's overshadowing presence, the divine voice singled out Jesus as "my Son, my Chosen" (Luke 9:35). No temporary booths could suitably enshrine the reality of this joy. The face of Moses had shone with the reflected glory of God (Exod 34:29); the son of Sirach assures us that Elijah appeared like a fire and his "word burned like a torch" (Sir 48:1). Neither proved to be the source of the glory he radiated. But Luke asserts of Jesus, as he prayed, that "the appear-

ance of his face changed, and his clothes became dazzling white" (Luke 9:29). For a brief moment Jesus let the disciples glimpse something of humanity enthroned at God's right hand.

In the first reading, taken from a Genesis account of the covenant God struck with Abraham, the glory of God appears as "a smoking fire pot and a flaming torch" (Gen 15:17) that passes between the severed parts of sacrificed animals. In doing so, God committed himself in the most solemn fashion to give the Promised Land to Abraham and his descendants. In the symbolism of ancient covenant making, God called down on himself, as it were, a curse (to be split like the animals) if he did not prove true to his promise. Of covenant breakers Yahweh said to Jeremiah "I will make [them] like the calf when they cut it in two and passed between its parts" (Jer 34:18). God proved true to that covenant by rescuing Israel from Egypt in the Exodus, as the verses omitted from this excerpt in the lectionary remind us: "I will bring judgment on the nation that they serve, and afterward they shall come out with great possessions" (Gen 15:14).

Paul, dealing with the challenges posed to his doctrine of liberty from the Mosaic Law by elements in the Philippian Christian community, looked beyond the sufferings of his present existence in the desert of travail. Paul looked forward to arrival in the Promised Land: "Our citizenship is in heaven, and it is from there that we are expecting a Savior, the Lord Jesus Christ" (Phil 3:20). Conformed to Christ's lowliness in this life, we look forward to being patterned on his glory in the next. On this Sunday or any Sunday we catch a glimpse of what is coming.

MONDAY OF THE SECOND WEEK OF LENT
Readings: Daniel 9:4–10; Luke 6:36–38

The first weekday of the second week of Lent picks up where the last weekday of the first week of Lent left off, featuring in the gospel passage from Luke the parallel to Matthew's summation of the new gospel of interior law: "Be perfect, therefore, as your heavenly Father is perfect" (Matt 5:48). Luke, however, underlines that perfection in terms of mercy, the quality of God who loves everybody, even those who profess to be God's enemies: "Be merciful, just as your Father is merciful" (Luke 6:36).

What are the parameters of mercy, the compassionate fellow-feeling that allows us to put ourselves in the position of those who have set themselves against us? Cynics would call such mercy foolishness, willingness to be duped and cheated and used. But God in Christ, having crossed the infinite divide that separates the Creator from the creature, provides in himself the incarnation of merciful compassion: God voluntarily assuming our human condition, reaching out to us who are weak and sinful, being taken as a sinner and put to death for the supposed blasphemy of claiming equality with God. Having urged us not to judge, not to condemn (Luke 6:37), Jesus himself was judged and condemned, learning at first hand what so many must suffer at the hands of their fellow human beings. Still, Jesus followed his own rule: "Forgive, and you will be forgiven" (Luke 6:37). On the cross, according to Luke, he turned in sympathy to a repentant thief: "Today you will be with me in Paradise" (Luke 23:43).

The first reading, somewhat loosely linked with the gospel passage, contains part of a prayer attributed to Daniel at the time of the Babylonian exile. On behalf of Israel, the upright Daniel takes on himself the guilt of his people: "Open shame, O Lord, falls on us, our kings, our officials, and our ancestors, because we have sinned against you" (Dan 9:8). The solidarity of the just Daniel with sinful Israel is meant, however, to evoke God's compassion: "To the Lord our God belong mercy and forgiveness" (Dan 9:9). The compassionate identification of Jesus with all of sinful humankind finds a foreshadowing in the solidarity of Daniel with God's people in exile for their sins.

TUESDAY OF THE SECOND WEEK OF LENT
Readings: Isaiah 1:10, 16–20; Matthew 23:1–2

Lyndon Baines Johnson was fond of quoting out of context, and in an antiquated translation, a verse from the prophecy of Isaiah that occurs in the first reading: "Come, let us reason together…" (Isa 1:18). This verse Johnson took as something of a theme song for his political wheeling and dealing, before and after he became president. The original context of the verse is an indictment by Yahweh of Israel for its many sins: "Hear the word of the Lord, you rulers of Sodom! Listen to the teaching of our God, you people of Gomorrah!" (Isa 1:10). Urging God's people to pay less attention to ritual (in verses unfortunately omitted in the lectionary: Isa 1:11–15), the prophet asks them to "rescue the oppressed, defend the orphan, plead for the widow" (Isa 1:17). Then comes the promise of forgiveness rather than reasoning together: "Come now, let us argue it out, says the Lord: though your sins are like scarlet, they shall be like snow" (Isa 1:18).

The gospel reading from Matthew reflects some of the same antagonism to a highly ritualistic faith that can be found in the omitted verses of Isaiah. But the school of Matthew, closer to the Pharisaic tradition than the schools of other evangelists, still sees some value in the purity of Pharisee religious practice: "The scribes and the Pharisees sit on Moses' seat; therefore, do whatever they teach you and follow it" (Matt 23:2–3). But once that is granted, Jesus and Matthew note that much of Pharisee practice falls short of Pharisee teaching: "But do not do as they do, for they do not practice what they teach" (Matt 23:3).

Among the items of Pharisee practice that Jesus deplores in Matthew's Gospel are a few customs that have survived into modern times in Catholic and other forms of Christian usage, and most notably the efflorescence of scholarly and clerical dignities and religious titles. "They love to have the place of honor at banquets and the best seats in the synagogues, and to be greeted with respect in marketplaces, and to have people call them rabbi. But you are not to be called rabbi (Matt 23:6–8). "Rabbi" was a title of academic prestige in learned Pharisee circles, a bit like "Professor" or "Doctor" in academe today. Jesus, whose attitude to the usage of that appellation is ambiguous elsewhere in the gospels (e.g., John 20:16–17), in this passage is portrayed as insisting that "you have one teacher, and you are all students" (Matt 23:8). The rejection of the title "Rabbi" may have been accepted in the early church, but its parallel title for Pharisaic scholars, "Father," has become widespread in the English-speaking world as a term of address for Catholic priests only since the nineteenth century. In many other European languages the term is reserved for a priest in a religious order rather than for the diocesan clergy, who had their own titles of dignity: M. le Curé, M. l'Abbé, Herr Pfarrer, Don, etc. All of these titles may possibly be tolerable, without going into various Monsignors, Milords, Your Excellencies and Your Eminences, if they do not prevent both the clergy and the laity from recognizing that "you have one Father—the one in heaven" (Matt 23:9).

WEDNESDAY OF THE SECOND WEEK OF LENT
Readings: Jeremiah 18:18–20; Matthew 20:17–28

Jeremiah had a difficult life. Called by God to deliver bad news (jeremiads) to Jerusalem (Jer 1:15–19), he found himself a more than usually despised prophet. The first reading for this Wednesday in Lent seems to look forward to Wednesday in Holy Week, "Spy Wednesday" as it is often called in English. Jeremiah and Jesus were both pursued by spies for those in power, people for whom Jeremiah was expendable. Religion could go on as usual without his discomforting tidings: "Instruction shall not perish from the priest, nor counsel from the wise, nor the word from the prophet" (Jer 18:18). They could find priests and sages and prophets more to their liking than the dour Jeremiah.

Matthew's Gospel, more indulgent to the memory of the disciples of Jesus than Mark's, ascribes to the mother of James and John, the sons of Zebedee, the request for her sons' advancement in the apostolic band: "Declare that these two sons of mine will sit, one at your right hand and the the other at your left, in your kingdom" (Matt 20:21). Mark seems to know that it was their own idea, not their mother's, or not just their mother's (Mark 10:35–37). This expression of ambition immediately follows in both gospels the third prediction of his passion, death and resurrection by Jesus (Mark 10:32–34; Matt 20:17–19), hardly an ideal time for talking about worldly advancement. Jesus is presented as seeming to know that the places at his right and left will be occupied by crucified thieves: "To sit at my right hand and at my left, this is not mine to grant, but it is for those for whom it has been prepared by my Father" (Matt 20:23). But he also told the sons of Zebedee that they too would share the cup of his suffering: "You will indeed drink my cup" (Matt 20:23).

When the rest of the apostolic band expressed their indignation at the wily maneuvering of James and John, Jesus reminded them that they were not called to be rulers in the Gentile fashion but servants of Yahweh, in the prophetic tradition. "Whoever wishes to be great among you must be your servant, and whoever wishes to be first among you must be your slave" (Matt 20:26–27). Their model in such selfless service must come from Jesus himself, who identified himself fully with the Servant of Yahweh sketched by Second Isaiah (Isa 42:1–4; 49:1–7; 50:4–11; 52:13–53:12). Some scholars have suggested that Second Isaiah, writing at the conclusion of the Babylonian exile, may have had the past sufferings of Jeremiah in mind when he sketched the prophetic portrait of the Servant whose proclamation of unpalatable truth brought him such grief. It may not be insignificant that Matthew's Gospel lists among the past prophets with whom the people identified Jesus not only the persecuted John the Baptist and Elijah but also Jeremiah (Matt 16:14).

THURSDAY OF THE SECOND WEEK OF LENT
Readings: Jeremiah 17:5–10; Luke 16:19–31

The Middle East, with its stark contrasts of fertile and arid landscapes, provides a natural image of contrasting moral states. The prophet Jeremiah and the author of the first Psalm both compare the upright person, who trusts in the Lord, to "a tree planted by water, sending out its roots by the stream" (Jer 17:8) or to "trees planted by streams of water, which yield their fruit in its season, and their leaves do not wither" (Ps 1:3). The unjust, however, are "like a shrub in the desert" (Jer 17:6) or "like chaff that the wind drives away" (Ps 1:4).

Jesus told a parable of two very different contemporaries, one of whom would normally be judged a just man rewarded by God with abundant wealth, the other a sinner punished with disease and poverty: the rich man and Lazarus. The difference between the two could be measured in terms of the distance between the banqueting table and the beggar's post at the gate. Both the rich man and the beggar died, and their situations were reversed in the age to come: "The poor man...was carried away by the angels to be with Abraham" (Luke 16:22), but the rich man got no further than a tormented grave where he found himself reduced to begging: "Father Abraham, have mercy on me, and send Lazarus to dip the tip of his finger in water and cool my tongue; for I am in agony in these flames" (Luke 16:24). The one who lived a hell on earth was now rewarded at the banquet with Abraham; the one who "dressed in purple and fine linen and who feasted sumptuously every day" (Luke

16:19) too late discovered what Lazarus had known for so many years at his gate.

But the time for begging and for almsgiving was past, and the fate of both men was sealed, as Abraham notes. "Between you and us a great chasm has been fixed, so that those who might want to pass from here to you cannot do so, and no one can cross from there to us" (Luke 16:26). The rich man, used to commanding service, asks that the ex-beggar go as a messenger to warn his five brothers of their impending fate. Too late for that as well. In any case, Abraham declares, "They have Moses and the prophets; they should listen to them" (Luke 16:29). The rich man pleads for the sending of a resurrected or perhaps a ghostly Lazarus: "If someone goes to them from the dead, they will repent" (Luke 16:30). Luke may well have been thinking about his impenitent Jewish contemporaries who did not respond to the church's message about the risen Jesus: "If they do not listen to Moses and the prophets, neither will they be convinced even if someone rises from the dead" (Luke 16:31). Fewer more vivid parables can be found in the New Testament of the contrasting moral outcomes of the just and the unjust.

FRIDAY OF THE SECOND WEEK OF LENT
Readings: Genesis 37:3–4, 12–13, 17–28;
Matthew 21:33–43, 45–46

Lenten Fridays begin to look in the direction of Good Friday. The first reading gives part of the masterly novella that dominates the final section of the Book of Genesis, the story of Joseph. Like its parallel version in the Qur'an, called "the most beautiful of all stories" (Qur'an 12:3), the story of Joseph illustrates God's providence for those he has chosen, even when they have to dwell in a foreign land and in difficult circumstances. Another and darker theme in the story surrounds the murderous hatred that motivates the sons of Jacob to plot to kill or at least eliminate one of their number: "Here comes this dreamer. Come now, let us kill him and throw him into one of the pits" (Gen 37:19–20). Reuben and Judah mitigate the sentence somewhat, condemning Joseph not to physical but to social death, selling him to Arabs ("Ishmaelites") as a slave. "For he is our brother, " Judah reasoned, "our own flesh" (Gen 37:27). The coolness of the argumentation cannot but remind us of the many centuries in which humankind sought to justify the inhumanity that was slavery. Psalm 105 sees in the affliction of Joseph an example of God's providence for Israel in Egypt: "When he summoned famine against the land, and broke every staff of bread, he had sent a man ahead of them, Joseph, who was sold as a slave" (Ps 105:16–17).

In the parable of judgment on Israel told by Jesus, the rebellious tenant farmers in a large vineyard refuse to pay his share to the vineyard proprietor. Not only do they refuse, but they set upon his slaves who bring them the message that they are to pay up: they "beat one, killed another, and stoned another" (Matt 21:35). Elsewhere in the scriptures Israel is often compared to the Lord's vineyard (Ps 80:9–17; Isa 5:1–7; Isa 27:2–6, etc.) and the prophets are often called God's slaves sent to deliver messages (Isa 42:1, etc.). It was not hard for the chief priests and the Pharisees to realize that Jesus "was speaking about them" (Matt 21:45), especially when the parable went on to specify that the tenant farmers not only maltreated the messengers of the proprietor but also his son: "But when the tenants saw the son, they said to themselves, 'This is the heir; come, let us kill him and get his inheritance'" (Matt 21:38).

Psalm 2, often interpreted as messianic in the Jewish tradition, speaks of the Lord and his anointed ruler in Jerusalem as his adopted son: "You are my son; today I have begotten you" (Ps 2:7). The inheritance promised to that royal son was immense: "Ask of me, and I will make the nations your heritage, and the ends of the earth your possession" (Ps 2:8). The plot to murder the son of the vineyard proprietor and seize his inheritance, like the plot of his brothers to murder or to enslave Joseph, both participate in the more general rebellion of humankind against the gentle rule of God's anointed king. Good Friday looms in the distance, four weeks away.

SATURDAY OF THE SECOND WEEK OF LENT
Readings: Micah 7:14–15, 18–20; Luke 15:1–3, 11–32

Many people who have had problematic relationships with one or both of their parents seem also to have problematic relationships with God. We first learn basic trust from our parents, and if through absence, removal or neglect we do not experience that basic trust even at a preconscious level (nursed at the breast, dandled in the arms), we may find it difficult to trust anyone later in life, including the Author of life.

God, of course, can always break through such barriers and disclose the divine trustworthiness to us in ways we might never suspect. For the people of Judah in the time of Micah (more or less a contemporary of First Isaiah in the eighth century B.C.), the reversals they were experiencing in their political fortunes were such as to suggest that God was a stern taskmaster punishing them for their transgressions. But the prophecy of Micah ends with the stirring exclamation and prayer that appears in part in the first reading: "Who is a God like you, pardoning iniquity and passing over the transgression of the remnant of your possession? He does not retain his anger forever, because he delights in showing clemency. He will again have compassion upon us; he will tread our iniquities under foot" (Mic 7:18–19).

The mercy of the God of Israel, a trait more central to the divine identity than justice or wrath, manifests itself most dramatically in a famous parable told by Jesus in a tradition handed on only by Luke. Usually called the story of the prodigal son, it should in fact be called the story of the prodigal father: a father whose relentless love for his wayward son gives us some clue to the overwhelming generosity of God's love for us, even when we sin. The elder son in the parable probably had much in common with those faithful Jews in the community of the disciples who resented the liberality with which Jesus himself welcomed into his company such disreputable people as recently repentant tax collectors and prostitutes. That resentment later on attached as well to Gentiles assimilated into the earliest Christian community without their submission to all the rigors of Jewish laws of diet and purity. In the name of the resentful upright, the elder son cries out against the prodigality of his father's love: "Listen! For all these years I have been working like a slave for you, and I have never disobeyed your command; yet you have never given me even a young goat so that I might celebrate with my friends" (Luke 15:29). But the prodigal father and a prodigal God insist on showing the utmost compassion to repentant sinners: "But we had to celebrate and rejoice, because this brother of yours was dead and has come to life; he was lost and has been found" (Luke 15:32).

Chapter 4

THE THIRD WEEK
OF LENT

THIRD SUNDAY OF LENT (A)
Readings: Exodus 17:3–7; Romans 5:1–2, 5–8; John 4:5–42

SLAKING THIRST

Andersonville in the state of Georgia preserves as a memorial park the prisoner-of-war camp where many Union soldiers died of thirst during the American Civil War. Around the older trees in the park deep holes remain where the desperate soldiers dug wells with their bare hands, hoping to discover sources of water. Thirst strikes the human imagination as a primal symbol of our deepest desires, perhaps because the experience of physical thirst so dramatically affects us. A human being can survive for a much longer time on a hunger strike than he or she can live without liquids.

The people of the Exodus discovered this shortly after they advanced into the southern reaches of the Sinai Peninsula in their flight from Egypt. "The people thirsted there for water; and the people complained against Moses and said, 'Why did you bring us out of Egypt, to kill us and our children and livestock with thirst?'" (Exod 17:3). Moses, already regretting the task he had undertaken at Yahweh's command, brought the problem to God's attention. He received precise instructions to strike a rock at Horeb (Sinai) from which water would flow. Yahweh specified the rock as the one where "I will be standing" (Exod 17:6), a curiously anthropomorphic reference to the divine presence. Paul, commenting on this and similar passages, saw in this rock where Yahweh stood a symbol of Christ. "All drank the same spiritual drink. For they drank from the spiritual rock that followed them, and the rock was Christ" (1 Cor 10:4).

Both Paul and the evangelist John meditated profoundly on Jesus as the source of the Spirit of God's holiness, the spring of life-giving water. Paul, in the second reading for this Sunday, proclaims that God's love for us has been poured out in each one of us "through the Holy Spirit that has been given to us" (Rom 5:5). The Gospel of John narrates how Jesus, at the Feast of Tabernacles, stood up in the Temple and exclaimed, "Let anyone who is thirsty come to me, and let the one who believes in me drink. As the scripture has said, 'Out of the believer's heart shall flow rivers of living water.' Now he said this about the Spirit, which believers in him were to receive" (John 7:37–39). Both of these texts illuminate the gospel passage for this Sunday, the dramatic dialogue between Jesus, the woman of Samaria and the choruses of disciples and townspeople.

The Gospel of Matthew gives the distinct impression that Jesus had forbidden his disciples to preach the good news to the people of Samaria (Matt 10:5), but Luke portrays Jesus as one more sympathetic to Samaritans (Luke 10:29–37; 17:11–19). The Samaritans, who still live in small numbers in areas of Palestine like Nablus and Gaza, trace their ancestry to the northern Israelites who were overrun by the Assyrians in 721 B.C. Although the Judeans accused them of hybridization with Gentile settlers or even of being Gentiles who took up Yahwism as a local cult (2 Kgs 17:24–28), the Samaritans maintain their fidelity to the Torah (the first five books of the Bible) and to the Yahwism therein inculcated. For many centuries before the time of Jesus, and up to the present among the surviving Samaritans, the sacrificial Yahwistic cultus of the Samaritans has centered on Mount Gerizim, not far from Nablus.

But the Samaritans had no regard for the later developments of the Yahwistic tradition found in Jerusalem and the Southern Kingdom, especially the teaching of the prophets and the pursuit of Wisdom. Furthermore, even before the Assyrian conquest of the Northern Kingdom, the Judean prophets had castigated the northern Israelites from whom the Samaritans trace their descent for resisting the centralization of Yahwistic cultus on Jerusalem. By the time of Jesus tensions between Jews and Samaritans were running high. The Jews of Galilee knew these tensions intimately, since they had to pass through Samaria whenever they traveled south to Jerusalem to fulfill their religious obligations at the Temple.

The Acts of the Apostles narrates a vigorous apostolate among the Samaritans by Philip, one of the Hellenistic Jewish evangelists from the Jerusalem church, followed by the imparting of the Holy Spirit to the Samaritan converts by the apostles Peter and John (Acts 8:1–25). Missionary openness to the Samaritans paved the way, according to the Acts of the Apostles, for the subsequent mission to Gentiles: "You will receive power," the ascending Jesus told his disciples, "when the Holy Spirit has come upon you; and you will be my witnesses in Jerusalem, in all Judea and Samaria, and to the ends of the earth" (Acts 1:8).

The encounter of Jesus with the woman of Samaria may well reflect John the evangelist's awareness of the missionary expansion of the Jewish-Christian community. Both Jesus and the woman came to Jacob's well to slake their thirst. But the woman, no model housewife, came at midday to perform a task normally associated with dawn. The reason for her late rising emerges in dialogue with Jesus. She had practiced the serial polyandry of Hollywood stars of a later century, "and the one you have now is not your husband" (John 4:18).

To distract him from her private life, the woman tried to divert Jesus to theological controversies, the cultic questions that

divided Samaritans and Jews. Jesus asserted quite clearly the cen-
trality of Jerusalem to the plan of salvation, but he also noted that
"the hour is coming, and is now here, when the true worshipers
will worship the Father in spirit and truth" (John 4:23). In the
aftermath of Pentecost, according to the Acts of the Apostles,
even the devotees of Yahweh at Mount Gerizim had the opportunity to drink to the full of the Spirit poured out in their hearts.
"Those who drink of the water that I will give them will never be
thirsty. The water that I will give will become in them a spring
of water gushing up to eternal life" (John 4:14). Filled with spirit
and truth imbibed from Jesus, the woman of Samaria broke out
of the disabilities imposed on her as a woman and a Samaritan
and proclaimed the good news to her fellow citizens.
Significantly, she "left her water jar" (John 4:28) behind her. She
would never be thirsty again.

Jesus shocked his disciples, as he had earlier shocked the
Samaritan woman, when they found him "speaking with a
woman" (John 4:27). Had they known as much about the
woman as she and Jesus did, they would have been even more
shocked. In breaking down the barrier between Jew and
Samaritan, Jesus also began to break down the barrier between a
pious rabbi and a woman of somewhat shady repute. Was Jesus
also breaking down the barriers between male and female? Saint
Paul, no ardent feminist, seems to have thought so: "There is no
longer Jew or Greek, there is no longer slave or free, there is no
longer male and female" (Gal 3:28). Such thoughts might have
prevented Paul's ecclesiastical advancement in a later era.

Jesus continued the tradition of Moses, who provided the
Israelites with water at Massah and Meribah (Ps 95:8). But for all
his fidelity to the Jewish tradition ("Salvation is from the Jews"
John 4:22), Jesus saw nonetheless the limitations of much that
was past in that tradition. "The hour is coming when you will
worship the Father neither on this mountain nor in Jerusalem"
(John 4:21). Ever since "God's love has been poured into our

hearts through the Holy Spirit" (Rom 5:5), there is no telling where we will worship God. God is not male or female, Jew or Samaritan. On the contrary, "God is spirit, and those who worship him must worship in spirit and truth" (John 4:24).

The first of three scrutinies of baptismal candidates takes place after the Liturgy of the Word on the third Sunday of Lent. Like the woman of Samaria, the candidates are called to drink a new and more satisfying water. In token of their repentance for past sins they are asked to kneel or bow during the Prayer for the Elect. The first of three exorcisms, prayers for deliverance from the besetting sins of our culture, is then pronounced by the celebrant.

He begins by asking God to slake the catechumens' thirst for God's Word, as Jesus did for the Samaritan woman. He prays that they too will experience a conversion of life. The celebrant then extends his hands over the candidates for baptism and calls on Jesus, the fountain of new life and teacher of all truth, to deliver the catechumens from all evil and impart to them God's peace.

THIRD SUNDAY OF LENT (B)
Readings: Exodus 20:1–17; 1 Corinthians 1:22–25; John 2:13–25

ICONOCLASTS AND ICONODULES

Leo the Isaurian, a Syrian Christian soldier with some simple ideas on art and theology, seized the imperial throne of Constantinople in A.D. 717. Having stemmed the Arab invasion of the Byzantine Empire that had been steadily advancing for more than eight decades, Leo and his military supporters blamed the previous defeats of the Byzantines on the fact that they venerated images of Jesus, Mary and the saints. Their Arab Muslim opponents shunned all human imagery in a religious context. Perhaps such anti-aesthetic puritanism had contributed

to the strength of the Arabs, or so Leo thought. Leo deposed Germanus I, the patriarch of Constantinople, and launched the iconoclastic heresy that bedeviled Eastern Christianity into the next century.

The ancient Israelite opposition to religious imagery, other than the purely verbal, arose from the fact that such plastic forms normally implied the worship of more than one god, the possibility that more than one transcendent being could hold sway over reality. Although Israel only came much later to the realization that no god but Yahweh held any power at all (see Isa 45), the Ten Commandments began their progress down that road to absolute monotheism. "I am the Lord, your God, who brought you out of the land of Egypt, out of the house of slavery; you shall have no other gods before me" (Exod 20:2–3). Fidelity to Yahweh, the God of Israel eventually seen as the only God, expressed itself concretely in keeping the terms of the covenant struck between God and humankind on Sinai.

But first and foremost, fidelity to God demanded the rejection of other gods and their idols: "You shall not bow down to them or worship them" (Exod 20:5). The Israelites, like every other child of Adam and Eve, fell prone to idolatry from time to time. It all began with our first parents' desire to make themselves into little gods, knowing good and evil (Gen 3:5). The veneration of images differs from the worship of idols in this important respect: the former is selfless, the latter self-centered. The idol worshiper wants to manipulate his or her god for selfish ends. The iconodule, to use a very technical term that means one who venerates images, loses himself or herself in contemplation of the imaged Transcendent.

With Solomon's construction of the Temple in Jerusalem, the temptation to worship Yahweh wrongly or manipulatively was in some sense curtailed. In another sense, however, the abolition of the local shrines to Yahweh (Dan, Bethel, Shiloh) handed the worship of Yahweh too easily over to the king and the levitical priesthood. By the time of Jesus, that priesthood, deeply compromised with the Romans and highly secularized, had reduced the Temple cultus to a major religious business. They had made the Temple itself something of an idol, a tourist attraction for Jew and Gentile alike. To such religious huckstering Jesus reacted strongly.

John's Gospel prefaces the public ministry of Jesus with his account of the cleansing of the Temple; the other three gospels locate it just before his passion. For John the cleansing of the Temple suggested the theme beloved by Hellenistic Jewish Christians like Stephen, that "the Most High does not dwell in houses made with human hands" (Acts 7:48). Elsewhere in John's Gospel Jesus tells the Samaritan woman at the foot of Mount Gerizim (where Samaritans worshiped) that "the hour is coming when you will worship the Father neither on this mountain nor in Jerusalem" (John 4:21). The relativization of the Temple, however, did not make Jesus a Unitarian Universalist. The Gospel of John makes it very clear that God still dwells among his people. "Jesus answered them, 'Destroy this temple, and in three days I will raise it up.' ...But he was speaking of the temple of his body" (John 2:19, 21). God still dwells among his people, even after the resurrection and ascension of the Lord in the sacramental bodying-forth of our incarnate Savior. The church itself, and especially its baptismal and eucharistic life, re-presents the Word made flesh in our midst. We venerate with incense the gospel book, the cross, the altar and the paschal candle as continuations of the temple of his body here and now.

Saint Paul, firing his first two salvos against his critics in the Corinthian Christian community, noted that neither Jews demanding signs of God's power to deliver them from bondage nor Greeks looking for philosophical insight or wisdom could make sense of a crucified messiah: "a stumbling block to Jews and foolishness to Gentiles" (1 Cor 1:23). At the center of our Christian churches we have, not a bowl of flowers nor an empty space, but a grisly instrument of capital punishment. We venerate the image of a crucified man, the temple of his body destroyed and raised in three days. Whether that image shows Jesus as the majestic Messiah enthroned on the cross or as the Suffering Servant twisted in his final agony, it demonstrates a central mystery of our faith. The Word of God became flesh once and forever. That incarnation of God as a fragile being of flesh and blood tears away the veil between earth and heaven, making possible both the most passionate concern for all flesh and blood and the most intimate involvement in imagining a world redeemed.

In Lent we are invited, not to become more ritualistic, but to become more human, more aware that God's new temple is a crucified and risen body, a body not unlike our own and not unlike the bodies of our fellow sufferers: victims of war, famine, disease, oppression, poverty, mental illness, loneliness. As worshipers at Yahweh's new temple we must turn our attention to their demands for human decency.

THIRD SUNDAY OF LENT (C)
Readings: Exodus 3:1–8, 13–15; 1 Corinthians 10:1–6, 10–12; Luke 13:1–9

WARNINGS

At Cashel in County Tipperary, once the royal and later the ecclesiastical center of Ireland's Province of Munster, a gravestone quotes in Latin the last verse of this Sunday's second reading: "If you think that you are standing, watch out that you do not fall" (1 Cor 10:12). Beneath the gravestone lie the mortal remains of a sixteenth-century clergyman, Myler McGrath, who managed rather deftly to straddle both sides of the great divide in Reformation Ireland. Less an ecumenist than an opportunist, McGrath held two episcopal sees at the same time, one Roman

Catholic and the other Church of Ireland (Anglican Communion). Those Church of Ireland or Roman Catholic Christians who may be tempted to judge Archbishop McGrath in later and less turbulent times are warned by Saint Paul's words not to rely on their own reputed uprightness. There is a little Myler McGrath in us all.

The scriptural readings for this third Sunday in Lent resonate with timely warnings. During the third week of this season the catechumens in early Christian Rome underwent their first scrutiny in preparation for baptism. Like the people of Israel in the era of the Exodus of whom Paul writes that "all were baptized into Moses in the cloud and in the sea" (1 Cor 10:2), the catechumens were about to be steeped into the death and resurrection (the Exodus) of Jesus. Would the beneficiaries of the new Exodus displease God as much as the generation that left Egypt under the guidance of Moses? "These things happened to them to serve as an example" (1 Cor 10:11). Catechumens and long-baptized, we have been warned.

Jesus used as warnings for all of us the example of the tragedies that befell some of his contemporaries: the savage slaughter of Galilean pilgrims in Jerusalem by Pontius Pilate and the death of eighteen innocent Jerusalemites in a structural collapse. Neither set of victims was any worse or any better than anyone else living in Galilee or Jerusalem at the time. Every death, difficult or easy, serves as a punishment for sin. Our human transitoriness might have been less painful had it not been for the grasping selfishness of sin that runs throughout the corporate history of the human race like a cancer. The slaughtered Galileans and the accident victims in the Siloam section of Jerusalem died deaths more tragic than do most people, but every death, even that of a saint, has about it an aspect of judgment, of finality. Ready or not, in death we enter into the presence of the absolute holiness of God. We recognize in that encounter not only our own woeful deficiencies but also the resplendent mercy of the judge who is also our deliverer.

The parable Jesus proposed in this context reminded his hearers that the few years of life allotted them (such as the three years of his public ministry) were meant to be an opportunity for spiritual transformation: *metanoia* in the Greek of the New Testament. If, like the barren fig tree of the parable, we bear no fruit year after year, we will eventually be cut down. "Why should it be wasting the soil?" (Luke 13:7). The vinedresser pleads with the vineyard owner to give the unproductive fig tree one more year while he hoes around the roots and manures the soil. Those who misread parables as allegories may use their ingenuity in figuring out what corresponds to hoeing and manuring in the Christian life.

The connection of the first reading with the other two in this Sunday's Liturgy of the Word is not obvious. The first reading for each third Sunday in Lent consists of a story about Moses, the promulgator of the Sinai covenantal law, beginning with the Ten Commandments formally given to the catechumens during this week. In this Sunday's excerpt from the Book of Exodus we learn how Moses received his calling to lead the Israelites from bondage into freedom. Although raised as an adopted child of Pharaoh's daughter, Moses fled from Egypt when his sense of solidarity with his fellow Israelites provoked him to slay an Egyptian who was beating a Hebrew. Taking refuge among the bedouin of north Arabia or the Sinai peninsula, Moses married into a bedouin family and tended his father-in-law's flocks. Driving these flocks across the wastes of Sinai, Moses came "to Horeb, the mountain of God" (Exod 3:1), another name for Mount Sinai, where he was later to receive the Ten Commandments. In this same place Moses first experienced the mysterious presence of God in a burning bush.

The first command Moses heard from God was a warning: "Come no closer! Remove the sandals from your feet, for the place on which you are standing is holy ground" (Exod 3:5). Before God commissioned Moses to lead the people, or revealed a personal sacred name, God demanded of Moses a physical reaction to the fact of God's numinous presence.

Much of our modern malaise with Christian morality, or even the Ten Commandments as we have been taught them, may well arise from our tendency to reduce the commandments of God to ethical norms dictated by common sense. Catechumens and the long-baptized both need to reflect on this Lenten Sunday on what a difference the command of God effects in our approach to morality. There is no rational reason why Moses should remove his sandals in the presence of the burning bush. But that little gesture concretized for that ancient Hebrew-Egyptian something of what it meant to confront the awesome majesty of God. Even if we Christians have been liberated from seeking our justification by performing works according to the Law, we still need from time to time to acknowledge the mysterious and demanding presence of God in our lives. Our God offers no rational self-definition, but merely presents that self in all its mystery: "I AM WHO I AM....This is my name forever, and this is my title for all generations" (Exod 3:14, 15).

During the third week of Lent, especially in Cycles B and C, the weekday readings for one day may be replaced by readings for the third Sunday in Cycle A, in particular the first reading (with two additional verses), Exodus 17:1–7 and the gospel reading, John 4:5–42. In places where catechumens are being prepared for baptism at Easter in the Rite for Christian Initiation of Adults, there may also be good liturgical reasons for using the readings for Sunday in Cycle A instead of those for the Sundays in Cycles B and C.

MONDAY OF THE THIRD WEEK OF LENT
Readings: 2 Kings 5:1–15; Luke 4:24–30

Leprosy can be cured at almost any stage, although all too often its progress is only noted when permanent damage has already been done to the extremities of those afflicted with it. Not everything described as leprosy in the Hebrew Bible (e.g., Lev 13:1–14:57) was genuine Hansen's disease, at is called today, taking its name from the Norwegian research scientist who determined its origins and made possible its remedy. But in ancient Israel almost any serious skin disease was classified as leprosy until proven otherwise, with the Temple priesthood serving as the public health service to verify infection or healing (Lev 14:2; Luke 17:14).

The story of Naaman, the leprous army commander from Aram (Syria) sent for healing to the prophet Elisha in the Northern Kingdom of Israel, resonates with wonderful human touches. Acting on a suggestion by an Israelite slave girl, the commander went with a letter from his sovereign to the king of Israel: "When this letter reaches you, know that I have sent to you my servant Naaman, that you may cure him of his leprosy" (2 Kgs 5:6). The Israelite king took this as an act of provocation, but Elisha the prophet assured him that he could handle the problem: "Let him come to me, that he may learn that there is a prophet in Israel" (2 Kgs 5:8). Although the Syrian general had been willing to act on the advice of an Israelite slave girl, he balked when the prophet, deliberately humiliating him, instructed him through a messenger that he should wash seven times in the Jordan. Naaman had been hoping for something a bit more exotic: "I thought that for me he would surely come out, and stand and call on the name of the Lord his God, and would wave his hand over the spot, and cure the leprosy!" (2 Kgs 5:11). Angry with Elisha, Naaman nearly decamped from Israel until his servants once again came to his rescue, telling him he had nothing to lose in trying the Jordan baths. Twice taking the advice of servants and humiliated by the arrogant Israelite prophet, Naaman was cleansed of his leprosy: "His flesh was restored like the flesh of a young boy, and he was clean" (2 Kgs 5:14).

Jesus cited the healing by Elisha of the Syrian Naaman rather than of any Israelite leper as a good precedent (along with the miraculous feeding by Elijah of the non-Israelite widow of Zarephath) for his own refusal to work miraculous healings in his hometown of Nazareth. Jesus made no friends with these words: "When they heard of this, all in the synagogue were filled with rage" (Luke 4:28). Jesus escaped the clutches of his fellow Nazarenes at this point, but, by a peculiar irony, when he was finally crucified his identity as a Nazarene was inscribed on his cross, at least according to John's Gospel (John 19:19). A prophet who worked miracles for a Syrian prepares the way for a messiah rejected by his own people and accepted by the nations.

TUESDAY OF THE THIRD WEEK OF LENT
Readings: Daniel 3:25, 34–43; Matthew 18:21–35

"Forgive us our debts," Jesus taught us to pray, "as we also have forgiven our debtors" (Matt 6:12), but as often as we utter his prayer, as often as we are forgiven by God, we still find it hard to forgive. The first reading for this Lenten weekday excerpts an eloquent prayer for forgiveness taken from one of the Greek supplements to the Book of Daniel, which begins as the story of a virtuous Jew and his companions who maintained their Jewish identity despite tyrannical threats against it in the court of the Babylonian despot Nebuchadnezzar who had conquered Jerusalem in 598 B.C. This edifying narrative was composed at the time of another and later attempt to wipe out Jewish religious differentness, the reign of the Greco-Syrian tyrant Antiochus IV

Epiphanes (175–163 B.C.). Meant to encourage Jews tempted to *hityavnut* ("Hellenization," i.e., secularism), the Book of Daniel recognizes that some have indeed compromised and need God's forgiveness. "In our day we have no ruler, or prophet, or leader, no burnt offering, or sacrifice, or oblation, or incense, no place to make an offering before you and to find mercy. Yet with contrite heart and a humble spirit may we be accepted" (Dan 3: 38–39).

The parable about forgiveness told by Jesus aims at contrasting the meanness of human forgiveness with the lavishness of God's forgiveness. The reign of God, not a divine tyranny but a divine amnesty, is compared to the extraordinary generosity of a monarch who forgave one of his ministers who owed him something approaching the national debt (ten thousand silver talents [Matt 18:24]). "Out of pity for him, the lord of that slave released him and forgave him the debt" (Matt 18:27). But the forgiven debtor learned nothing in the process. Coming upon a lesser official who owed him a hundred *denarii*, about three or four months' wages, the minister demanded repayment, even having this minor debtor imprisoned.

Other servants of the reign reported this callous behavior to the king, who promptly reversed his cancellation of the unforgiving minister's debts: "Should you not have had mercy on your fellow slave, as I had mercy on you?" (Matt 18:33). Jesus underlined the theme for any who might have missed the point: "So my heavenly Father will also do to every one of you, if you do not forgive your brother or sister from your heart" (Matt 18:35).

WEDNESDAY OF THE THIRD WEEK OF LENT
Readings: Deuteronomy 4:1, 5–9; Matthew 5:17–19

Catechumens in the early Roman church underwent scrutinies in preparation for baptism at Easter during the third week of

Lent, including an examination of their understanding of the Ten Commandments. The readings for the liturgy of this Lenten Wednesday reflect that tradition, without reproducing the Ten Commandments already set forth in the first reading for the Third Sunday in Cycle B. The first reading, however, comes from the first discourse of Moses in the Book of Deuteronomy, a discourse in which the patriarch speaks in general about the importance of those commandments he has delivered to Israel from God: "What other great nation has a god so near to it as the Lord our God is whenever we call to him? And what other great nation has statutes and ordinances as just as this entire law that I am setting before you today?" (Deut 4:7–8).

Jesus, especially in the traditions preserved by Matthew, refuted the suggestion that he had abolished the Law of Moses completely. But, on the other hand, Matthew had to recognize that the attitude of Jesus to that Law was not the same as the attitude of observant Pharisees contemporary with him. For Jesus, the Law needed perfecting in the reign of God that was coming. "Do not think that I have come to abolish the law or the prophets; I have come not to abolish but to fulfill" (Matt 5:17). Translated and excerpted like that, *fulfill* can be misunderstood to mean "obey," pure and simple. But the verses that follow this gospel excerpt indicate that Jesus intended his disciples to internalize and perfect the Law of Moses. Not only must his disciples refrain from murder, as the fifth commandment bids them; they must even restrain in themselves the anger that can, at its extreme, overflow into acts of murder (Matt 5:21–26). Not only must they avoid adultery, as the sixth commandment bids them, but they are to avoid the lustful desire that leads to it (Matt 5:27–30).

The practitioners of such fulfilling or perfecting of the Law of Moses will take the leadership roles in the reign of God that is coming, while those who fall short in such fulfilling or perfecting of the Law, even though they make it under the wire into the era of God's reign, will attain only a lesser status: "Whoever breaks one of the least of these commandments, and teaches others to do the same, will be called least in the kingdom of heaven; but whoever does them and teaches them will be called great in the kingdom of heaven" (Matt 5:19).

THURSDAY OF THE THIRD WEEK OF LENT
Readings: Jeremiah 7:23–28; Luke 11:14–23

Religion apparently annoys God from time to time, to judge from occasional passages in the Bible. Through Amos, Yahweh declared that he had seen enough of ritual sacrifices: "I hate, I despise your festivals, and I take no delight in your solemn assemblies. Even though you offer me burnt offerings and grain offerings, I will not accept them" (Amos 5:21–22). Similar sentiments were expressed through Isaiah (Isa 1:11–17). In each case Yahweh expressed a preference for social justice over solemn assemblies and elaborate liturgy. Such an interpretation of true religion lies just beneath the surface of the passage from Jeremiah used in the first reading for this Lenten weekday, although the omission of the two verses just before this excerpt makes it less clear than it might be. Prophesying on God's behalf to late seventh-century B.C. Jerusalemites overconfident that the Lord would preserve the Temple and its devotees from foreign conquest, Jeremiah uttered words shocking by religious standards of a later period: "In the day that I brought your ancestors out of the land of Egypt, I did not speak to them or command them concerning burnt offerings and sacrifices" (Jer 7:22).

What about the passage about holocaust in Leviticus (Lev 1:1–17)? Such ritual regulations may possibly reflect priestly developments of a period much later than that of Jeremiah, when the ritual life of postexilic Israel tended to overshadow its prophetic tradition. Jeremiah was more interested in fidelity to the basic covenant struck between Yahweh and Israel: "Obey my voice, and I will be your God, and you shall be my people; and walk only in the way that I command you, so that it may be well with you" (Jer 7:23). Jeremiah, speaking like all prophets on God's behalf, noted that his contemporaries "walked in their own counsels, and looked backward rather than forward" (Jer 7:24).

In the gospel passage taken from Luke Jesus complained of similar obduracy on the part of his contemporaries who charged that his exorcisms of mentally disturbed people, whose illnesses were then defined as diabolic possession, derived from "Beelzebub, the ruler of the demons" (Luke 11:15). Jesus pointed out the absurdity of the notion that the personified power of evil would contribute to the miraculous conquest of evil. "If Satan also is divided against himself, how will his kingdom stand?" (Luke 11:18). Like Jeremiah, Jesus faced a hostile audience, hostile enough to twist the meaning of his healing and liberating action into the very opposite of its evident significance. On such people, elsewhere said to be those who sin against the Holy Spirit by denying the goodness of his miracles (Mark 3:28–30), Jesus uttered a resounding condemnation: "Whoever is not with me is against me, and whoever does not gather with me scatters" (Luke 11:23).

FRIDAY OF THE THIRD WEEK OF LENT
Readings: Hosea 14:2–10; Mark 12:28–34

In case anyone missed the point of the scrutinies on the Ten Commandments suggested by the earlier liturgical readings of this third week of Lent, the church pairs in this Friday's readings two biblical passages that sum up response to God's commandments in terms not of obedience but of love. The prophet Hosea, the eloquent voice of God's love for the unfaithful Israelites of the Northern Kingdom in the eighth century B.C., used his own experience of an unfaithful and adulterous wife as a paradigm for what his fellow citizens were doing to the God who loved them. At the conclusion of the prophecy of Hosea, the author urged the Northern Kingdom to eschew adulterous political and military alliances with Gentile powers and their idolatrous cults: "Assyria shall not save us; we will not ride upon horses; we will say no more, 'Our God,' to the work of our hands" (Hos 14:3). The prophet, speaking in God's words, assured the Northern Kingdom in lush arboreal imagery that its true fruition would develop out of reliance on Yahweh: "I will be like the dew to Israel; he shall blossom like the lily, he shall strike root like the forests of Lebanon" (Hos 14:5).

In Mark's Gospel the enunciation by Jesus of the great commandment, two commandments combined as one, is presented rather differently than it is by Matthew and Luke. In Matthew's Gospel, it is presented as an answer to a hostile lawyer attempting to test Jesus (Matt 22:35). In Luke's Gospel, it is the conclusion reached by the lawyer himself and approved by Jesus (Luke 10:25–28), but then the lawyer wanted to quibble about the definition of *neighbor* and elicited from Jesus the parable of the good Samaritan (Luke 10:29–37). In Mark's account, however, Jesus simply combined the commandment from Deuteronomy to love God above all else (Deut 6:4–5) with the commandment from the Holiness Code of Leviticus to "love your neighbor as yourself" (Lev 19:18). The scribe who asked him, "Which commandment is the first of all?"(Mark 12:28), congratulated Jesus on so combining these two texts. Jesus, in turn, congratulated the scribe for the insight implicit in his congratulations: "You are not far from the kingdom of God" (Mark 12:34). An insight into the cousinship between the Pharisee and Christian ethical traditions can be gleaned from this exchange of congratulations, one too often missed in Matthew's and John's hostile presentations of the Pharisees, more the product of late first-century A.D.

controversies between church and synagogue than of early first-century events in the life of Jesus.

SATURDAY OF THE THIRD WEEK OF LENT
Readings: Hosea 6:1–6; Luke 18:9–14

Most of us sinners fall from grace through human weakness: anger, lust, envy, covetousness, sloth, gluttony overcome us and we give in. But there are some people who sin because of their human strength: the self-righteous. Living fairly controlled lives, they look down on those more prone to the grosser temptations than they. It is easier for the humanly weak to recognize their need for repentance than it is for the proud upright. At the end of a week dominated by the commandments of God, but especially the great commandment to combine the love of God with the love of neighbor, the liturgy for this Saturday takes a long look at those of us who fail to live up to these high ideals. Hosea, eloquent as ever in his role as God's spokesman, urges not only the Northern Kingdom (Ephraim) of the eighth century B.C. but also the Southern Kingdom (Judah) to repent of their idolatrous flirtations with the gods of the nations. "What shall I do with you, O Ephraim? What shall I do with you, O Judah? Your love is like a morning cloud, like the dew that goes away early" (Hos 6:4). But Hosea, like Jeremiah, reminded the Israelites that what God wanted was not more ritual sacrifice but something more substantial: "For I desire steadfast love and not sacrifice, the knowledge of God rather than burnt offerings" (Hos 6:6).

Luke alone preserved the parable told by Jesus about the Pharisee and the tax collector, the latter better known as "the publican," a term that makes him sound, not entirely unsuitably, like a tavern keeper in Ireland or Britain. According to Luke, Jesus aimed the parable at "some who trusted in themselves that they were righteous and regarded others with contempt" (Luke

18:9). This parable, more than anything else in the New Testament, contributed to the creation of the small-p pharisee out of the big-P Pharisees, a lay movement of vigorous Torah piety. As in every good movement, there were, undoubtedly, some who took it to extremes, but the conflict between Jewish Christians and Jewish Pharisees only became particularly acute after the destruction of the Temple in A.D. 70, a disaster that spelled the doom of the priestly class and the Zealots as well, leaving the Pharisees and their rabbinical experts as the main intellectual and spiritual force within Judaism. But at an earlier period in the same century Paul found allies among the Pharisees in the Sanhedrin against the Sadducees (Acts 23:6–10).

Both the Pharisee and the tax collector entered into alien territory, something of a Sadducee preserve, when they both "went up to the temple to pray" (Luke 18:10). But the Pharisee presumed, in his self-righteousness, that he could stand up straight in God's presence: "God, I thank you that I am not like the other people: thieves, rogues, adulterers, or even like this tax collector" (Luke 18:11). One can only sympathize with God having to hear out prayers that begin like that. Then the tax collector, a despised agent of Roman imperial domination of Palestine, had his chance to approach God: "God, be merciful to me, a sinner!" (Luke 18:13). Jesus drew a conclusion from this parable that must have startled his contemporaries, so accustomed to admiring Pharisee uprightness. The tax collector may not have been very just in his past dealings, but the humility of his prayer for mercy meant that he "went down to his home justified" (Luke 18:14), while the Pharisee did not. The core of Paul's teaching about justification of a person by God's graciousness rather than by works according to the law lies hidden in this parable: "But now, apart from the law, the righteousness of God has been disclosed…the righteousness of God through faith in Jesus Christ for all who believe" (Rom 3:21–22).

Chapter 5

THE FOURTH WEEK
OF LENT

FOURTH SUNDAY OF LENT (A)

Readings: 1 Samuel 16:1, 6–7, 10–13; Ephesians 5:8–14; John 9:1–41

CHRISTENING

We sometimes refer to baptism as christening, the making of a Christian through sacral anointing. Early church sources also sometimes called baptism enlightenment, the bestowal of the light of Christ. The basic sacrament of Christian initiation involves the participants in various rites that serve as metonyms to designate the whole mystery: washing or dipping in water, anointing with blessed oils, presentation with a burning candle. All three images for this sacrament play a role in the gospel passage for this Sunday, as well as in the other readings, following an ancient tradition of the Roman church that situated the second scrutinies (examinations) of candidates for Easter baptism in the fourth week of Lent. For those of us long-baptized, this Sunday renews in us our baptism into Christ, the source of our light.

The christening or anointing of King David occupies center stage in the first reading, an abbreviated account of how Samuel found the one whom he was to anoint as Saul's replacement not in the older sons of Jesse but in the youngest, a youth assigned the lowly task of tending his father's sheep. The exaltation of the lowly as God's anointed one (messiah) began with God's choice of tiny

Israel as his Chosen People and continued in the divine election of David. God's ways are not the ways of mortals: "The Lord said, 'Rise up and anoint him; for this is the one'" (1 Sam 16:12).

The gospel passage, best proclaimed in dramatic fashion as are the passion narratives in Holy Week, tells the story of a man blind from birth whose eyes were opened by Jesus. In the process of his enlightenment, however, the man underwent many trials, much scrutiny. Jesus prepared him for this with an initial anointing: "He spat on the ground and made mud with the saliva and spread the mud on the man's eyes" (John 9:6). Anointing with mud made from spittle symbolically suggests that the opening of the blind man's eyes will not be an unmixed blessing.

The evangelist insists that the name of the pool in which the anointed blind man was to wash, Siloam, means "Sent" (John 9:7). In John's Gospel Jesus plays the role of God's emissary, "he whom God has sent" (John 3:34). Eventually Jesus sent his disciples forth as he had been sent: "As you have sent me into the world, so I have sent them into the world"(John 17:18). Baptized into the one whom God sent, the newly enlightened man had to face a series of interrogations. To the first of these scrutinies ("Is not this the man who used to sit and beg?" [John 9:8]), he replied, quite simply, "I am the man" (John 9:9). This English translation does not catch quite accurately the irony implied in the Greek of the gospel text. Besides the many usages of these words in conjunction with such predicates as Life and Light, in the passage just before this gospel story Jesus had been hounded out of the Temple for blasphemy when he declared that "before Abraham was, I am" (John 8:58). Only God can say of himself, "I AM WHO I AM" (Exod 3:14). The formerly blind man steeped in the baptismal waters of the one who has been sent becomes, as it were, another Christ, another person to be hounded out of the Temple.

The Gospel of John was written at the end of the first century A.D. when Jewish Christians, at first tolerated in the larger Jewish community, were excommunicated by the rabbinical leadership of Pharisee convictions, the only religious authority that survived the Roman destruction of Jerusalem. This excommunication of the Jewish Christians is probably reflected in John's portrayal of the blind man's pusillanimous parents who admitted to their questioners that he was their son and that he had been blind since birth, but who referred the interrogators to their son for any further information on how he came to his sight. "His parents said this because they were afraid of the Jews; for the Jews had already agreed that anyone who confessed Jesus to be the Messiah would be put out of the synagogue" (John 9:22).

The man born blind gradually learned what it meant to be anointed with mud made from spittle. Undeterred by the lack of parental support or the hostility of the religious leadership, this man, who had still never actually seen Jesus face to face, spoke up boldly for the one who had enlightened him: "If this man were not from God, he could do nothing" (John 9:33). For this profession of faith in the Lord he had never seen, the man born blind suffered symbolic excommunication: "'You were born entirely in sins, and are you trying to teach us?' And they drove him out" (John 9:34).

The excommunication of Jewish Christians as heretics from the synagogue communities of the Middle East after A.D. 85 colors the account of the altercation between the newly sighted man and the Jewish authorities in Jerusalem. What has sometimes been called the anti-Semitism of John's Gospel may rather reflect the inner-Jewish struggles of those late first-century Jews who accepted Jesus as Lord and Messiah and those who did not. Any victim of persecutions—religious, racial or those based on gender or disabilities—can understand the rising frustration of the formerly blind man as his interrogations continued: "Why do you want to hear it again? Do you also want to become his disciples?" (John 9:27).

Anointing with mud made from spittle began a process of downward mobility for the man born blind, reduction from beggary to the status of an outcast. Precisely in this abasement he came to an insight into Jesus beyond merely physical vision: "Do you believe in the Son of Man?" (John 9:35). Previously, the man born blind had accepted Jesus as a healer, a prophet, a just man, someone who came from God. Now, face to face with Jesus, the newly sighted man was asked to affirm his faith in the humanity of the one who came from God. The community of the beloved disciple was familiar with those who questioned the flesh-and-blood reality of Jesus (1 John 4:2; 2 John 7). A spiritual version of Jesus, Jesus made into a principle or a manifestation of God, appealed in ancient times to those embarrassed by the gospel portrait of one who smeared mud made from spittle on the eyes of a man born blind.

To this man, baptized into the one whom God has sent, Jesus finally showed himself: "I came into this world for judgment so that those who do not see may see, and those who do see may become blind" (John 9:39). Saint Paul, one struck blind by Jesus in order to make him see (Acts 9), never forgot the difference between light and darkness. Quoting what may be an ancient baptismal hymn, he (or another author in the school of Paul) urged the Ephesians to open their eyes to the light of Christ: "Sleeper, awake! Rise from the dead, and Christ will shine on you" (Eph 5:14) The fourth Sunday of Lent bids us to look beyond the trials of this-worldly Christian existence to the resurrected future when we will see Christ our Light face to face.

Once again the candidates for baptism at Easter undergo a scrutiny that includes an exorcism. Like the man born blind, they need the power and encouragement that only the Lord can give. The celebrant begins by praying to God the Father to free those chosen for baptism from blindness and falsehood and introduce them into the kingdom of truth and light. Then the celebrant imposes his hands on each of the candidates for baptism before extending his hands over all of them and praying to Jesus to free all from the yoke of slavery to sin and darkness and give them the courage that the man born blind had to profess their faith.

FOURTH SUNDAY OF LENT (B)
Readings: 2 Chronicles 36:14–17, 19–23; Ephesians 2:4–10; John 3:14–21

CAT FAITH

In the Hindu devotional tradition, two types of loving faith *(bhakti)* are differentiated: monkey faith and cat faith. In monkey faith the devotee personally clings to the Lord, exerting every human effort to hold on to God like an infant monkey clinging with all its might to its mother. In cat faith the devotee exerts little or no personal effort and simply allows himself or herself to be carried by the Lord as a kitten allows itself to be carried by its mother, hanging limply from the mother's teeth. Both attitudes are types of loving faith, but cat faith evidences the most complete reliance on a loving Lord, a Lord willing to save us by the scruff of our necks.

The second reading in this Lenten Sunday's Liturgy of the Word provides us with a New Testament version of cat faith. It suggests that God is the principal agent in our salvation, our rescuer from the death that is sin. The Epistle to the Ephesians sums this up in a succinct phrase: "by grace you have been saved" (Eph 2:5). Grace, also called favor, is a way of characterizing the magnanimous intervention by God in our cycle of death-dealing lovelessness. Like the mother cat of Hindu devotionalism, God "raised us up with him [Christ] and seated us with him in the heavenly places" (Eph 2:6). We do not rescue or save ourselves from sin: "This is not your own doing; it is the gift of God" (Eph 2:8). We dangle from God's teeth, rescued from the jaws of everlasting death.

This has been the history of grace for a long time. Just when we were tempted to think that we had come of age and could rely on our own moral and spiritual strength, God lets us realize who alone can save us from annihilation. The first reading, taken from the conclusion of the Chronicler's narrative, presents the tragic end of Israelite hopes for self-rule (as opposed to Yahweh-rule) through the House of David. Judah and Jerusalem, David's capital, "were exceedingly unfaithful" (2 Chr 36:14) until God "brought up against them the king of the Chaldeans" (2 Chr 36:17). Even the center of Yahwistic worship, the Temple in Jerusalem, was razed to the ground. In such devastation the Chronicler saw punishment for neglect of the Sabbath rest, a theme adapted from Jeremiah 25:11–12.

But the Chronicler, like Jeremiah, did not conclude on such a mournful note. The last verses of the Chronicler and the first verses of the Book of Ezra are nearly identical. If God reduced Jerusalem to ashes for its infidelity, God restored it to its rightful glory through the instrumentality of Cyrus, king of Persia. What a strange mother cat God provided in Cyrus! Both Second Isaiah (see Isa 45) and the Chronicler are agreed that this Persian world-conqueror played a providential role in God's plan for history.

The discourse in the gospel reading, although attributed by the lectionary to Jesus in dialogue with Nicodemus, seems more likely to be a monologue of Jesus or even a homily about Jesus emanating from an evangelist in the school of the beloved disciple. Three times in the Gospel of John the death, resurrection and ascension of Jesus are referred to collectively as his being "lifted up" (John 3:14; 8:28; 12:32, 34). In this, the first occurrence of the image, the passage of Jesus through death into glory is compared to the curious and somewhat magical antitoxin Moses offered to the Israelites afflicted by fiery serpents in the desert. "Just as Moses lifted up the serpent in the wilderness, so must the Son of Man be lifted up, that whoever believes in him may have eternal life" (John 3:14–15).

The fiery serpents symbolically concretized the persistent nagging and discontent of God's people as they "spoke against God and against Moses" (Num 21:5). To cure them of this affliction, Moses, at Yahweh's command, made a fiery serpent of bronze and raised it on a standard. "Whenever a serpent bit someone, that person would look at the serpent of bronze and live" (Num 21:9). Is it too modern to suggest that the transformation of their nagging and discontent into an idol enabled the Israelites to confront the fact that they were trying to manipulate the God who saved them from Egyptian bondage?

The gospel reading suggests that Jesus is the bronze serpent of the new Exodus, the antitoxin for the rebelliousness that has alienated us from God. Our faith in the crucified, risen and ascended Jesus—the Son of Man lifted up before our eyes—can rescue us from darkness and bring us into the light. Like the bronze serpent, Jesus concretized our human weakness and "emptied himself, taking the form of a slave, being born in human likeness. And being found in human form, he humbled himself and became obedient to the point of death—even death on a cross" (Phil 2:7–8). Lifted up, Jesus became the mother cat rescuing us from the jaws of death. Saved by the scruff of our necks, we hang in faith from his teeth.

The gospel reading continues with some of the most moving words in the New Testament, and especially with the verse referred to on a placard at nearly every televised football and basketball game in the United States, John 3:16: "God so loved the world that he gave his only Son, so that everyone who believes in him may not perish but may have eternal life." Like the bronze serpent, Jesus transforms the very reality that plagues us, death. At the tomb of Lazarus Jesus wept (John 11:35), moments before he was to raise Lazarus from the tomb. Even with the imminent hope of resurrection, death pained Jesus as it pains us, and especially the death of a friend. God sent Jesus into our world of death to deliver us, as he delivered Israel from Egypt and the Jews from Babylon. In raising up the cross before our eyes, God offers to each one of us the chance to conquer death as Jesus conquered death, by going through it with faith. "Those who believe in him are not condemned; but those who do not believe are condemned already, because they have not believed in the name of the only Son of God" (John 3:18).

FOURTH SUNDAY OF LENT (C)
Readings: Joshua 5:9, 10–12; 2 Corinthians 5:17–21;
Luke 15:1–3, 11–32

A NEW BEGINNING

On the fourth Sunday of Lent, called *Laetare* ("Rejoice") Sunday from the first Latin word in its entrance antiphon, the church breaks the violet monotony of this liturgical season and allows sacristy haberdashers to outfit the celebrants of the Sunday Eucharist in rose-colored vestments. On this Sunday in the Roman basilica of the Holy Cross in Jerusalem, the Holy See has often awarded the Vatican equivalent of the Oscar, the Golden Rose, to an eminent benefactor of the church. In recent years, the Golden Rose has more typically gone to institutions dedicated to the sanctification of the faithful, such as the various shrines of the Virgin Mary.

In the year 1096, when the awarding of the Golden Rose was already considered an ancient institution, Pope Urban II, one year after he called for the First Crusade, bestowed the Golden Rose on his fellow Frenchman, Fulk IV of Anjou, better known as Fulk the Surly. In 1887, the Holy See gave the Golden Rose to a 24-year-old American heiress, Mary Gwendoline Caldwell, who had recently donated $300,000 toward the founding of the Catholic University in Washington, D.C. Some years later the former Miss

Caldwell, by then the Marquise des Monstiers-Merinville, renounced Catholicism. The history of Fulk the Surly and Catholic University's early benefactress may have prompted the change from awarding the Golden Rose to individuals.

The Liturgy of the Word for this Laetare Sunday looks forward in joyful anticipation to the new beginning that the paschal mystery affords humanity. In the first reading, excerpted from the Book of Joshua, the Exodus comes to an end when the generation that had wandered in the desert for nearly forty years underwent circumcision as an entry rite into the celebration of the Passover. Although the prebiblical significance of circumcision is obscure, the Book of Exodus insists that only the circumcised may participate in the Passover meal: "If an alien who resides with you wants to celebrate the passover to the Lord, all his males shall be circumcised" (Exod 12:48). The Passover meal narrated in the first reading seems to be the second in history but the first taken in the Promised Land of Canaan. It marked a new beginning for God's people once God had removed "the disgrace of Egypt" (Josh 5:9) from them.

Saint Paul, defending his embattled ministry in the correspondence he conducted with the Christians of Corinth, expatiates in the second reading on the difference that the death and resurrection of Jesus made in Paul's life and can make in anyone's life. Just before this passage Paul had written that "from now on, therefore, we regard no one from a human point of view" (2 Cor 5:16). As Saul of Tarsus, Paul had once persecuted Jesus in the body of his disciples. But the crucified and risen Messiah Jesus, overwhelming Paul on the road to Damascus, had changed him radically. The oneness of Jesus with God and the oneness of Jesus with those who put their faith in him became the central pillars of Paul's newfound faith. Paul had experienced in himself, first of all, but then in others as well, whether Jew or Gentile, the possibility of a new beginning in life. "If anyone is in Christ, there is a new creation: everything old has passed away; see, everything has become new" (2 Cor 5:17). Paul saw himself as the ambassador of this new state, this new creation.

The gospel parable, unique to Luke's account of Jesus, was originally aimed at those respectable contemporaries of Jesus who resented his fraternizing with tax collectors and other disreputable types. In our own day, the parable addresses all those who profess themselves shocked by the easy absolution available in Catholic confessional practice for the truly repentant. More significantly, within the borders of Catholicism, the parable of the two sons and their prodigal father contains a lesson for those who query the greater facility with which invalid marriages are dissolved by some American diocesan tribunals. The older brother lurking inside each one of us bridles at the liberality of God and of the church in dealing with human fallibility.

Hollywood has always liked the parable of the prodigal son. The "prostitutes" (Luke 15:30) mentioned in passing by the protesting elder son suggested endless possibilities for alluring spectacles of debauchery, great Babylonian feasts of revelry vaguely reminiscent of something from *A Thousand and One Nights*. The point of the story, however, gets lost in the Hollywood process. The parable, as opposed to the movie, stars the father and his elder son, the former prodigal in his loving forgiveness and the latter niggardly in his refusal to accept the reconciliation of his brother.

The younger son has too long preoccupied the human imagination, perhaps because the lives of sinners are more interesting than the lives of prigs. Hollywood could never make a costume epic out of the life of the older brother who admitted that the life of virtue had proven very dull: "For all these years I have been working like a slave for you, and I have never disobeyed your command" (Luke 15:29). But it is the older brother who makes the point of the parable Jesus addressed to his pious critics. Luke's fellow Christians in the first century may also have understood the parable as significant in assessing the relationship between Jewish Christians who still observed the Mosaic Law and the "younger" Gentile Christians who felt no compunction about the dietary regulations of the Old Covenant.

The generous father of both sons welcomes back the youth who squandered his inheritance but does not repudiate the older son who protests the father's prodigality yet remains faithful to the father. "Son, you are always with me, and all that is mine is yours" (Luke 15:31). The restoration of the son who "was dead and has come to life," who "was lost and has been found" (Luke 15:32), does not invalidate the fidelity of the older son. Everything the father has, the full riches of both the Old Covenant and the New, is available for the Jewish Christian, even if life may seem to be easier for the Gentile Christian.

The younger son, restored to the father's household, must make a new beginning in the life of fidelity. Reconciled to God, younger son and older son must work out together their reconciliation with each other.

During the fourth week of Lent, especially in Cycles B and C, the weekday readings for one day may be replaced by the gospel reading for the fourth Sunday in Cycle A preceded by Micah 7:7–9. In places where catechumens are being prepared for baptism at Easter in the Rite for Christian Initiation of Adults, there may also be good liturgical reasons for using the readings for Sunday in Cycle A instead of those for the Sundays in Cycles B and C.

MONDAY OF THE FOURTH WEEK OF LENT
Readings: Isaiah 65:17–21; John 4:43–54

The funerals of children surely rank highest on the list of terrible duties a priest may have to perform; only the family of the dead child suffers more. The first reading for this Monday in the middle of Lent, taken from Third Isaiah, celebrates God's creation of "new heavens and a new earth" (Isa 65:17), probably a way of speaking about the new realities the Jews experienced when they returned from the Babylonian exile to the Promised Land and its sacred capital, Jerusalem. In the Book of Revelation this new Jerusalem is exalted on high, not located in the Middle East (Rev 21:1–2). But for Third Isaiah and his contemporaries, the land of their ancestors in the vicinity of the Jordan was new to them. In celebrating this newness, the prophet associated it with the end of all infant death in a new Jerusalem: "No more shall there be in it an infant that lives but a few days, or an old person who does not live out a lifetime" (Isa 65:20).

The gospel reading for this weekday begins an unbroken series of gospel readings from John for the rest of the Lenten weekdays until Wednesday of Holy Week; all of the previous Lenten weekday gospels have been taken from Matthew, Mark and Luke. Picking up where the gospel ends for the Third Sunday of Lent (A), John narrates how Jesus returned from Samaria to Galilee, revisiting Cana "where he had changed the water into wine" (John 4:46). The second sign Jesus performed at Cana served as something of a signal that he had instituted the new heavens and a new earth for which Third Isaiah yearned.

The royal official whose infirm son he healed at a distance was most likely a courtier of Herod Antipas; "Herodians" were, somewhat like tax collectors for the Roman Empire, compromised Jews, at very best, dependents of a mixed Jewish-Idumean puppet dynasty. Whatever the religious identity of this royal official before this time, the critical illness of his son drove him to seek out Jesus as a worker of signs. Not happy with faith dependent on miraculous signs, Jesus used the opportunity to rebuke his contemporaries: "Unless you see signs and wonders you will not believe" (John 4:48). Nevertheless, Jesus took pity on this man of very pragmatic faith and healed his son at a distance, not compromising his own Jewishness in the process by entering the home of this compromised man. Despite this affront, the royal official went beyond his previous faith in miracles to faith in the incarnate Word: "The man believed the word that Jesus spoke to him" (John 4:50). Arriving home a day later, the court official found his son restored to health at "the hour when Jesus had said to him, 'Your son will live'" (John 4:53).

TUESDAY OF THE FOURTH WEEK OF LENT
Readings: Ezekiel 47:1–9, 12; John 5:1–3, 5–16

The Bethesda Fountain in New York City's Central Park, featuring a great bronze angel descending into the topmost part of the fountain, takes its name from a spurious verse in John's Gospel, missing from the best manuscripts, that has also been eliminated from the gospel passage for this Lenten weekday. Evidently the verse is a scribal annotation or gloss explaining a popular belief associated with miraculous healing thought to take place at the pool near the Sheep Gate in ancient Jerusalem: "For an angel of the Lord went down at certain seasons into the pool, and stirred up the water; whoever stepped in first after the stirring of the water was made well from whatever disease that person had" (John 5:[4]). As we enter into the second half of our Lenten preparation for the sacrament of baptism or its devotional renewal, the church presents us over three days in the middle of this fourth week of Lent with a somewhat baptismal sign performed by Jesus on a Sabbath day and its consequences.

For an unlucky disabled man never quick enough to make it first into the pool "when the water is stirred up" (John 5:7) Jesus himself provided a wellspring of healing: "Stand up, take your mat and walk" (John 5:8). The story of the healing is immediately complicated by the gospel's mention that this healing, and the command by Jesus that the man who had been disabled for thirty-eight years should take up his mat and walk, took place on the Sabbath, the weekly day of rest when such activities, blandly defined as servile labor, should not be performed. The newly mobile man found himself the object of obloquy by the officially religious: "It is the sabbath; it is not lawful for you to carry your mat" (John 5:10). The accused had no idea who Jesus was and with what authority he had commanded him to stand, take up his mat and walk away. Later in that day, Jesus met him in the Temple and urged him to avoid some unspecified sins in his past. Curiously ungrateful, or possibly religiously naïve, the newly healed man informed the religious guardians that it was Jesus who had cured him. The gospel writer tells us that "the Jews started persecuting Jesus because he was doing such things on the sabbath" (John 5:16).

The first reading for this day, a lush symbolic vision of the restored Temple after the Babylonian exile, portrays that Temple as a source of abundant fresh water in a previously desiccated area. Like the rivers that watered the Garden of Eden (Gen 2:10–14), the streams flowing from the Temple refresh a new creation. "Wherever the river goes, every living creature that swarms will live" (Ezek 47:9). Restorative water—healing the disabled, refreshing the desiccated—suggests baptism in a Christian context, whatever may have been its significance in its original setting. The argument about the authority of Jesus over the Sabbath rest is handled in the gospel excerpts for the next two weekdays.

WEDNESDAY OF THE FOURTH WEEK OF LENT
Readings: Isaiah 49:8–15; John 5:17–30

God comes to us in the readings for this weekday as both Mother and Father. The maternal imagery for God arises in the excerpt from Second Isaiah that serves as the first reading. Celebrating the return of the Jewish exiles from Babylon to Jerusalem, the prophet compares the rescuing God of Zion (the

Temple mount and Jerusalem more generally) to a tender-hearted mother. "Can a woman forget her nursing child, or show no compassion for the child of her womb? Even these may forget, yet I will not forget you" (Isa 49:15). God rescuing the Jews from Babylon acted as their judge in the sense that this term has in the Book of Judges, the stories of heroes and heroines who acted on God's behalf as deliverers of Israel from the hands of its enemies.

Jesus, challenged by those religious critics who only saw a violation of the Sabbath rest in the healing he had just performed for the cripple at the Pool of Bethesda, left them thunderstruck with the boldness of his assertion of a right to violate the Sabbath rest on a par with God whom he boldly called his Father. "My Father is still working, and I also am working" (John 5:17). The Sabbath rest was mandated as an imitation of God: "Six days you shall labor and do all your work. But the seventh day is a sabbath to the Lord your God" (Exod 20:9–10). But even God, according to extrabiblical Jewish tradition, breaks the Sabbath rest to cause rainfall, to give life to the newborn and to judge the dead. From this notion flows much of what follows in today's gospel, one of the clearest expressions of what later theology called the consubstantiality or shared equal reality of Jesus with God the Father.

Jesus spoke of himself as God's Son, but a Son who was, as it were, apprenticed to and imitating his Father: "The Son can do nothing on his own, but only what he sees the Father doing; for whatever the Father does, the Son does likewise" (John 5:19–20). Among those things that God the Father does which Jesus imitated was raising the dead: this passage from John's Gospel looks forward to the seventh and most spectacular of the signs worked by Jesus, the raising of Lazarus (John 11). Not only did Jesus hold the keys of life and death, but he asserted that God had handed over to him the duty of judging the dead: "The Father judges no one but has given all judgment to the Son, so that all may honor the Son just as they honor the Father" (John 5:22–23). Also, like God, Jesus had the power to give life, even on the Sabbath. "Just as the Father has life in himself, so he has granted the Son also to have life in himself" (John 5:26). Jesus left his opponents stunned by the power of the legal defense he made on his own behalf: "As I hear I judge; and my judgment is just, because I seek to do not my own will but the will of him who sent me" (John 5:30). This trial imagery continues tomorrow.

THURSDAY OF THE FOURTH WEEK OF LENT
Readings: Exodus 32:7–14; John 5:31–47

It sometimes seems more important in the United States for big-time malefactors to have a good team of lawyers (one will never do) than to have a good case. The lawyer as superstar can sometimes seem to be able to get the devil off with a slap on the wrist. The people of Israel had a particularly good lawyer in Moses, especially during the Exodus. He got them off the hook more than once with God. In the first reading for this Lenten weekday Moses had a tough case to argue before the heavenly bench: Israel under Aaron's guidance had lapsed into idolatrous worship of a golden calf during a prolonged absence of Moses, even calling the animal image Yahweh (Exod 32:4–5). "Now let me alone," Yahweh told Moses, "so that my wrath may burn hot against them and I may consume them; and of you I will make a great nation" (Exod 32:10). Flattering as the divine offer to begin his holy people again with Moses only may have been, the patriarch resisted the suggestion, even bringing in some other lawyers to help him argue his case for Yahweh to continue to choose Israel: "Remember Abraham, Isaac and Israel, your servants, how you swore to them by your own self, saying, 'I will multiply your descendants like the stars of heaven'" (Exod 32:13).

Jesus admitted the truth of the charge, as yesterday's gospel excerpt put it, that "he was not only breaking the sabbath, but was also calling God his own Father, thereby making himself equal to God" (John 5:18). But he denied that he was the only one testifying on his behalf, never sufficient for establishing a case. Jesus cited other witnesses to his divine status, and therefore the legitimacy of his doing the work of God on the Sabbath. First and most important of the witnesses for Jesus was God the Father, who enabled him to perform miraculous signs like the healing of the disabled man at the Pool of Bethesda. John the Baptist had testified for Jesus as well, but the divine witness outshone that fragile but very human "burning and shining lamp" (John 5:35). "I have a testimony greater than John's. The works that the Father has given me to complete, the very works that I am doing, testify on my behalf that the Father has sent me" (John 5:36). Not only the miracles Jesus could perform on behalf of the Father testified to his authenticity as the Son of the Father, but the Father himself testified to his Son. But, alas, all too many of his contemporaries could not listen to such testimony. "You have never heard his voice nor seen his form, and you do not have his word abiding in you, because you do not believe him whom he has sent" (John 5:37–38).

The image of Moses as the lawyer for Israel returns in the gospel reading, but he has turned now into a potential prosecuting attorney, not a defender of Israel. "Do not think that I will accuse you before the Father; your accuser is Moses, on whom you have set your hope" (John 5:45). The infidelity of Israel to the Law of Moses, so much lamented by the prophets, showed that God's Chosen People were unworthy of the lawyer who had so ardently defended them in God's presence at the time of the Exodus. "If you believed Moses, you would believe me" (John 5:46). *Believe* is too weak a word in English to translate what the gospel says in Greek: "If you had kept faith with Moses you would have kept faith with me."

FRIDAY OF THE FOURTH WEEK OF LENT
Readings: Wisdom 2:1a, 12–22; John 7:1–2, 10, 25–30

Good Friday once more looms on the horizon, the shadow of the cross touching this Friday with its mysterious luminosity. The first reading comes from the Book of Wisdom, a moving portrait of a just Jew persecuted for his uprightness. The Book of Wisdom, written in Greek by an Alexandrian Jew just a few decades before the time of Jesus, possibly refers to upright Jews persecuted not by hostile Gentiles but by nonobservant fellow Jews who have given themselves over rather totally to self-indulgent Hellenistic ways in Alexandria. Just before the main part of this excerpt these secularized voluptuaries exhort each other: "Let no flower of spring pass us by. Let us crown ourselves with rosebuds before they wither" (Wis 2:7–8). But epicureanism was not enough for these worldly types; they felt impelled to persecute whoever opposed their life style. "Let us lie in wait for the righteous man, because he is inconvenient to us and opposes our actions; he reproaches us for sins against the law and accuses us of sins against our training" (Wis 2:12). These secularized Jews seem to have known what they were rejecting, the status of Israel as the child of God. They hate the just one for reminding them of the covenant, and their hatred turns to violence. "Let us condemn him to a shameful death" (Wis 2:20).

In the gospel excerpt, rather too little of the seventh chapter of John, Jesus is seen going up to Jerusalem , despite threats to his life, to participate privately in the celebration of the Feast of Booths *(Sukkoth)*. While in Jerusalem for the feast, however, Jesus changed his mind about the privacy he had sought and began to preach openly in the Temple precincts, not far from the Pool of Bethesda where he had cured the disabled man on a Sabbath day and made such extravagant claims to divine status (John 5:1–47). The crowd realized how controversial that visit to Jerusalem had been, as well as an earlier one when he cleansed the Temple of religious commerce at Passover and claimed that he could raise up a Temple in three days if this one were destroyed (John 2:13–25). As a result, the crowds were amazed at the audacity of his return to the holy city. "Is not this the man whom they are trying to kill? And here he is, speaking openly, but they say nothing to him!" (John 7:25–26).

The crowd proceeded to speculate about the messianic status of Jesus, a topic on which he had been noticeably reticent or even reluctant, fleeing a recent attempt to proclaim him king (John 6:15). But the fickle crowd, presuming they know the origins of Jesus in Galilee (John 7:41) and that they would not know the origins of the messiah, withdrew from their messianic hopes. Jesus took them up ironically on their certitude about his origins: "You know me, and you know where I am from. I have not come on my own. But the one who sent me is true, and you do not know him. I know him, because I am from him, and he sent me" (John 7:28–29). These words, among the boldest Jesus ever spoke, effectively questioned what the Jews presumed they certainly knew: the one true God. Jesus, claiming an origin directly from that God, went even further than he had when he claimed the divine right to judge and give life on the Sabbath. The evangelist remarks that, despite this provocation, "no one laid hands on him, because his hour had not yet come" (John 7:30). The hour of Jesus, the hour of his entrance as Son into the glory of the Father (John 13:1), would come in the events of Good Friday.

SATURDAY OF THE FOURTH WEEK OF LENT
Readings: Jeremiah 11:18–20; John 7:40–53

The reasons for which we may be tempted to despise people are often trivial: accent, the accidents of personal appearance, either too much or too little refinement of manners. In John's

Gospel, Nathanael, from the rather insignificant village of Cana in Galilee, as we learn later in the gospel text (John 21:2), thought little of Jesus because he came from another insignificant town in Galilee: "Can anything good come out of Nazareth?" (John 1:46). Eventually Nathanael learned to revise his opinion of Nazarenes (John 1:47–51). But the crowds gathered for the Feast of Booths in Jerusalem were convinced that the future messiah or anointed king of Israel would have to come from the same unlikely village from which David took his origins, Bethlehem in Judea. John's Gospel tradition may not know anything about the birth of Jesus at Bethlehem, a motif preserved by both Matthew (Matt 2:4–8) and Luke (Luke 2:1–5), but if the Johannine evangelist did know these traditions, the reactions of the crowd to the apparent Nazareth and Galilee origins of Jesus were particularly ironic. "Surely the Messiah does not come from Galilee, does he? Has not the scripture said that the Messiah is descended from David and comes from Bethlehem, the village where David lived?" (John 7:41–42).

Despite these popular doubts about the messianic or prophetic status of Jesus, the popularity of this Galilean preacher and healer in Jerusalem and the Temple precincts was such that the Temple guards felt unable to arrest him in public. The forces promoting the arrest, apparently an alliance of the usually antagonistic "chief priests and Pharisees" based in Jerusalem (John 7:45), despised not only Jesus but the crowds who listened with such attention to his preaching. "Has any one of the authorities or of the Pharisees believed in him? But this crowd, which does not know the law—they are accursed" (John 7:48–49). Nicodemus, a leading Pharisee member of the Sanhedrin and something of a secret disciple of Jesus (John. 3:1–10), spoke up at this point, pointing out that the Law of Moses did not allow condemnation of anyone without a fair hearing. The anti-Galilean prejudices of the Jerusalem elite, Sadducee and Pharisee, lie revealed in their retort to Nicodemus: "Surely you are not also from Galilee, are you? Search and you will see that no prophet is to arise from Galilee" (John 7:52).

The first reading derives from a lament of Jeremiah's about earlier conspirators in Jerusalem, just as prejudiced against unpopular prophetic truth: "But I was like a gentle lamb led to the slaughter. And I did not know it was against me that they devised schemes" (Jer 11:19). Jeremiah and Jesus both had to look to God for their justification when the religious elite and the crowds in Jerusalem turned against them.

Chapter 6

THE FIFTH WEEK
OF LENT

FIFTH SUNDAY OF LENT (A)
Readings: Ezekiel 37:12–14; Romans 8:8–11; John 11:1–45

THE GIVER OF LIFE

Pranayama, the control of breath, plays a central role in the techniques of yoga, the spiritual and physical discipline so characteristic of India. Although a yogic posture like the lotus position, frequently adopted before the practitioner's knees are ready for it, more typically symbolizes meditative concentration, breath control contributes much more to inducing the physical calm necessary for interior liberation. Not only in India, but in many parts of the world, breath has appealed to the human imagination as an ideal symbol not only for interiority but also for the real but invisible realm of the Transcendent. God's Spirit, the human spirit, breath and wind are all designated by the same word in the Hebrew Bible. The labored breathing of the dying and the wailing first breath of the newborn associate breath with life and especially with the interior space where mortal beings experience their dependence on a life-giving God.

The prophet Ezekiel, a priest of the Jerusalem Temple destroyed in the Babylonian conquest of 587 B.C., imaged exiled Israel as a valley of dry bones, a graveyard of all human hope. Only the creative breath of God could restore these dry bones to life, just as God's breath enlivened Adam at the creation (Gen 2:7). The first reading contains only the last three verses of

Ezekiel's vision. In resurrecting scattered Israel, Yahweh promised to breathe into the Chosen People his own life: "I will put my spirit within you, and you shall live" (Ezek 37:14).

Saint Paul had much to say about God's Spirit and the human spirit in the eighth chapter of the Epistle to the Romans. The short excerpt in the second reading emphasizes the contrast between flesh and spirit, a contrast not to be understood in Platonic terms. Flesh for Paul connoted much the same thing as dry bones for Ezekiel: lifelessness. Platonists misconstrue Paul if they make him into an angelistic despiser of the human body. The faith-filled Christian lives his or her baptized life as one enlivened by the Spirit Jesus poured out on his disciples: "If the Spirit of him who raised Jesus from the dead dwells in you, he who raised Christ from the dead will give life to your mortal bodies also, through his Spirit that dwells in you" (Rom 8:11). The Spirit of God and the Spirit of Christ share the work of giving life in this passage from Paul. The credal affirmation that the Holy Spirit is also the Lord, the giver of life, derives in part from the church's meditation on this Pauline teaching.

At first appearance the gospel story of how Jesus raised Lazarus from the dead may not seem to continue the theme of the life-giving Spirit of God and of Christ. But closer examination of the text yields some surprises. After Mary approached Jesus with her stark declaration that "if you had been here, my brother would not have died" (John 11:32), the evangelist writes that Jesus "was greatly disturbed in spirit and deeply moved" (John 11:33). Later, when he came to the tomb of Lazarus, the evangelist states that Jesus was "again greatly disturbed" (John 11:38). In each case the translation is too bland. In each of these instances the Greek text suggests that Jesus quite literally groaned or snorted in his spirit or in himself. What did such a description imply? Strange as it may seem, the evangelist seems to be saying that Jesus was enraged: snorting in the spirit at death, chafing at the bit to deal a deadly blow to the Evil One,

groaning in indignation and anger with himself for allowing Martha, Mary and Lazarus to experience this tragedy. After all, as the evangelist earlier reminded us, "Jesus loved Martha and her sister and Lazarus" (John 11:5). And yet he had delayed in coming to their rescue so that other disciples might come to believe (John 11:15). A mystic of a later period once remarked, with the boldness only possible for such a person, that it was no wonder God had so few friends if he treated those whom he loved so badly.

Enraged in the spirit, Jesus shouted at the entrance of the tomb where Lazarus was decaying: "Lazarus, come out!" (John 11:43). To the present day, the resulting wonder has marked the section of modern east Jerusalem (once suburban Bethany) where all this happened. Palestinian Arabs who live there call the neighborhood *al-'Azariyah*, Lazarus Town. Egeria, the late fourth-century pilgrim and diarist from Spain who toured the Christian holy places of the Middle East, reports that a procession took place on the Saturday before Palm Sunday to Bethany where Jesus raised Lazarus from the tomb. The Greek-speaking churches revere the memory of Lazarus and his two sisters, Martha and Mary, complementing the narratives about them in Luke and John with the story that Lazarus eventually became a bishop in Cyprus. In any case, it was at the tomb of Lazarus, shortly before his own death and resurrection, that Jesus entered into fierce struggle in the spirit with the power of death, taking one hostage from the jaws of the grave. Unlike the risen Jesus, however, Lazarus "came out, his hands and feet bound with strips of cloth, and his face wrapped in a cloth" (John 11:44). He had to be untied. When Jesus rose from the dead, he left the grave cloths behind, forever triumphant over death, naked as the newly created Adam.

With the raising of Lazarus, however, a battle had begun. In the verses that follow the gospel passage, the evangelist narrates how the Sanhedrin resolved, in the wake of these events, to eliminate both Jesus and the unfortunate Lazarus (John 11:46–53; 12:9–11). Becoming a friend of Jesus cost Lazarus, Martha and Mary dearly. Christian tradition remembers the three of them as saints, made holy by their painful closeness to this friend who loved so much, who gave his Spirit, who raised to life.

The third and final scrutiny of candidates for baptism takes place after the Liturgy of the Word. After the bidding prayers, the celebrant prays to God the Father to liberate these baptismal candidates from the power of the Evil One and the realm of death and introduce them into the life of grace that reaches its completion in the resurrection. Once again imposing hands on each candidate in turn, the celebrant calls on Jesus, who raised Lazarus from the tomb, to give these catechumens the life of the sacraments and a share in the glory of resurrected life after death.

FIFTH SUNDAY OF LENT (B)
Readings: Jeremiah 31:31–34; Hebrews 5:7–9; John 12:20–33

HEART TO HEART

Ancient Israel was a tiny country wedged uncomfortably in the space between bellicose superpowers. As such Israel had to master the art of diplomacy, working out treaties with those encroaching empires. Neutrality like that of modern Switzerland, combined with total reliance on Yahweh, might have served Israel better than international entanglements, as several of the prophets had urged. It is dangerous for mice to dance with elephants. Not surprisingly, religious thinkers in Israel envisioned their nation's relationship with the sovereignty of God in much the same way that they conceived of its relationship with the rulers of Egypt, Assyria and Babylon. Yahweh was always the senior partner, the suzerain, in the diplomatic treaty or covenant between Israel and its God. In the Books of Exodus and Deuteronomy, in particular, Moses acted as the shuttle diplomat between the contracting parties.

With the collapse of the last remnant of Judean territorial sovereignty before the Chaldeans in 587 B.C., the prophet Jeremiah reached the conclusion that the old covenant worked out between God and Israel at the time of the Exodus had broken down. The first reading for this Sunday's Liturgy of the Word enshrines the prophet's hope for a new covenant that Yahweh would work out "with the house of Israel and the house of Judah" (Jer 31:31) at some future time. This passage from Jeremiah, referred to several times in the New Testament and quoted in its entirety in the Epistle to the Hebrews (Heb 8:8–12), gives its title to the written account of the new covenant, the New Testament.

What did Jeremiah understand as *new* in God's covenant? Whereas the Mosaic covenant had been inscribed on tablets of stone, the new covenant, God assures the prophet, would be written on human hearts. The central covenantal formula—"I will be their God, and they shall be my people" (Jer 31:33)—is the key to both the old and the new covenants, but the means for effecting the terms of these two covenants differ. External law in the old covenant had proven inadequate to restrain human sinfulness. In the new covenant, God would enter into human consciousness in a new way: "I will put my law within them, and I will write it on their hearts" (Jer 31:33).

The gospel reading from John contains the third and final reference in the fourth Gospel to Jesus being "lifted up" (John 12:32). The first two usages of that term throw light on the third. Something of a euphemism for public execution, the phrase is employed for the first time in what seems like an exhortation by the evangelist after the encounter between Jesus and Nicodemus: "Just as Moses lifted up the serpent in the wilderness, so must the Son of Man be lifted up, that whoever believes in him may have eternal life" (John 3:14–15). The lifting up of the bronze serpent cured those who looked at it (Num 21:8–9); the lifting up of Jesus on the cross would provide the ultimate healing of all humankind. In the second instance, Jesus himself is reported as having used the term in controversy with his opponents in the Temple precincts. In this instance the lifting up in execution coincides with lifting up as exaltation to the divine throne: "When you have lifted up the Son of Man, then you will realize that I am he" (John 8:28).

The universal sovereignty that Jesus assumed in his death, resurrection and ascension is dramatically portrayed in this Sunday's gospel passage. Greeks, presumably proselyte Gentiles, approached Jesus through Greek-speaking disciples. As he entered into the final Passover of his life, Jesus discerned in the approach of these Gentiles an end and a beginning. For Jesus the approach of Gentiles spelled an end to his personal apostolate among the people of Israel and an end, as well, to his limited mortality as one male Jew of the first century. He also sensed in the advent of these Greeks the beginning of the wider messiahship into which he would enter through the portals of death: "The hour has come for the Son of Man to be glorified" (John 12:23).

As a frail human being like ourselves, Jesus feared the dissolution of his individuality that such lifting up, such glorification necessarily entailed. This gospel passage has rightly been described as John's equivalent of the synoptic gospel accounts of the agony in the Garden of Gethsemane. The new covenant, before it was written in your heart or mine, was seared into the consciousness of Jesus of Nazareth: "Now my soul is troubled. And what should I say? — 'Father, save me from this hour?' No, it is for this reason that I have come to this hour" (John 12:27).

The second reading, from the Epistle to the Hebrews, picks up this theme of the personal agony Jesus suffered in entering into his kingdom. The author of this theological meditation insists that God heard his Son's prayer and delivered him from death, or better, brought him through death into resurrection and enthronement with God. "Although he was a Son, he learned obedience through what he suffered; and having been made perfect, he became the source of eternal salvation for all who obey him" (Heb 5:8–9).

The new covenant written on our hearts was written first, and in letters of fire, on the heart of Christ. Psalm 51 asks God to create "a clean heart" (Ps 51:10) in each one of us. The clean heart and right spirit that we pray for in this Psalm are the heart and spirit of the messiah who willingly became a servant. "Whoever serves me must follow me, and where I am, there will my servant be also" (John 12:26). If we allow the messiah who became a servant to take possession of our hearts, we will have no further need, as Jeremiah prophesied, for law in our relationship with God: "No longer shall they teach one another, or say to each other, 'Know the Lord,' for they shall all know me, from the least of them to the greatest, says the Lord; for I will forgive their iniquity, and remember their sin no more" (Jer 31:34).

FIFTH SUNDAY OF LENT (C)
Readings: Isaiah 43:16–21; Philippians 3:8–14; John 8:1–11

REDEEMER

Although the Qur'an forbids faithful Muslims to have anything to do with "the filth of Satan's work" that consists of "wine, lotteries, idols and divining with arrows" (Qur'an 5:90), not a few Muslims over the fourteen centuries of Islamic history have taken an interest in all of these temptations. Even if divining with headless arrows, a pre-Islamic Arab method of fortune-telling, has fallen out of fashion, other techniques of divination derived from the armory of such practices that long antedates the rise of Islam survive among Muslims. Along with many other religious people throughout the world, and especially Christians and Hindus,

Muslims pay more attention than it deserves to astrology, an inheritance from the ancient Magians of Mesopotamia and Iran.

Yet another method of divination, geomancy, although derived from non-Islamic sources, continues in various parts of the Islamic world, especially in Muslim areas of Africa. Whereas astrology groups human fortunes in the twelve houses of the Zodiac, geomancy discovers the unknown in sixteen basic configurations of four even (2) and odd (1) digits. Each of these sixteen configurations may be combined with any other, making 256 different signs of geomancy. Either through a manual of interpretation or through memorized traditional verses, a geomantic diviner connects with each of these 256 signs, usually drawn in a random fashion in sand or dust, something that is supposedly hidden or unknown.

Most scripture scholars have suggested that Jesus, when called upon to pass judgment on the woman caught in adultery, was either playing for time or imitating the gestures of a magistrate writing out his sentence. Those who are familiar with the ancient Middle Eastern practice called in Arabic *khatt al-raml* ("sand-writing") may wonder whether Jesus wasn't teasing the scribes and the Pharisees with their superstitious fear that he might be able to expose their hidden sins by means of divination.

Just as it takes, in the words of an old song, two to tango, adultery cannot be accomplished without two partners, at least one of them married. In the gospel reading for this Lenten Sunday, very possibly an excerpt from the Gospel of Luke transferred into the text of John, a woman caught in the act of adultery is dragged into the presence of Jesus. Where was her partner in sin? Selective enforcement of the law has a long history. The scribes and the Pharisees who brought this woman to Jesus were using the occasion to embarrass him either into repudiating the Law of Moses, which mandated capital punishment for adultery (Lev 20:10), or defying Roman law, which apparently denied the Jews the *jus gladii*, the right to inflict the death penalty (see John 18:31).

As in the dilemma posed to him on paying tribute to Caesar, Jesus chose neither alternative. In his majestic silence as he drew in the sand, he prepared the scribes and the Pharisees for an ironic command: "Let anyone among you who is without sin be the first to throw a stone at her" (John 8:7). Jesus never contradicted the Law of Moses on adultery. Implicitly, however, he questioned the procedure by which the adulterous woman had been caught in the act and her lover had not. Silent again, he returned to writing in the sand. One by one the woman's accusers withdrew, ashamed of their stratagems.

With all the witnesses of the alleged crime gone, the case against the woman collapsed. The early church, stricter than Jesus in its disciplinary practice toward adulterers, may have been embarrassed by this refusal of Jesus to judge, even if he exhorted the woman to avoid this sin in the future (John 8:11). In a time and place when film and fiction, at least, presume that casual adultery plays a large part in the popular imagination, we need to notice that Jesus never condoned adultery. He exercised the prerogative of judge and deliverer in the Hebrew tradition, rescuing this hapless woman from her accusers, redeeming her from a seemingly hopeless predicament.

The first reading, taken from Second Isaiah, celebrates "a new thing" (Isa 43:19) achieved by Yahweh. Israelite faith had for centuries centered on the Exodus, Yahweh's deliverance of the people of Israel from Egyptian bondage. But the author of this canticle insists that the return of the Jews from Babylon constituted a miracle even more significant: "Do not remember the former things, or consider the things of old" (Isa 43:18). The deliverance of the Chosen People from Babylon, like the deliverance of the woman caught in adultery, demonstrated the superabundant nature of God's mercy, God's willingness even to outdo himself in forgiving love.

Saint Paul, writing to the Philippians, assured that Gentile community wondering whether they might not be better advised to adopt the Mosaic Law along with their faith in Jesus as Lord and Christ, that he himself, "a Hebrew born of Hebrews" (Phil 3:5), considered his own deep rootedness in the Jewish tradition "as loss because of the surpassing value of knowing Christ Jesus my Lord" (Phil 3:8). This passage must be read in the context of Paul's intense yearning for the reconciliation of his own people with God in Christ. But even a devout Jewish Christian had to realize that strict observance of the commandments still could not deliver flesh and blood from the weight of sin. Justice, in Paul's terms, could only derive from the innocent Jesus who died for the sin of Adam. "The power of his resurrection" (Phil 3:10) redeems both Jew and Gentile and bids us to sin no more.

During the fifth week of Lent, especially in Cycles B and C, the weekday readings for one day may be replaced by the gospel reading for the fifth Sunday in Cycle A preceded by 2 Kings 4:18–21, 32–37. In places where catechumens are being prepared for baptism at Easter in the Rite for Christian Initiation of Adults, there may also be good liturgical reasons for using the readings for Sunday in Cycle A instead of those for the Sundays in Cycles B and C.

MONDAY OF THE FIFTH WEEK OF LENT
Readings: Daniel 13:1–9, 15–17, 19–30, 33–62; John 8:1–11 [A & B] **or** *John 8:12–20 [C]*

If the fifth Monday in Lent could be given a peculiar name of its own in English, on the model of the Wednesday of Holy Week called "Spy Wednesday," "Entrapment Monday" might do nicely. Both the readings center on stories of attempts at legal entrapment, especially when the gospel narrative of the woman caught in adultery (John 8:1–11) is proclaimed on the Mondays following the fifth Sundays of Lent in the A and B Cycles. But even on

Monday following the fifth Sunday of Lent in Cycle C, the alternative gospel passage, the immediate sequel to the story of the woman caught in adultery in the Vulgate and many other editions of John's Gospel (and the sequel to this past Saturday's gospel in other manuscripts), fits in quite well with the courtroom motif.

In the darkness of the legal conspiracy against him, Jesus proclaimed boldly that he was "the light of the world. Whoever follows me will never walk in darkness but will have the light of life" (John 8:12). The Pharisees returned to the accusation that he was his own only witness in the trial they were surreptitiously trying to conduct. Jesus took them on directly: "Even if I testify on my own behalf, my testimony is valid , because I know where I have come from and where I am going, but you do not know where I come from or where I am going" (John 8:14). He then insisted on his union with the Father as a co-witness: "I testify on my own behalf, and the Father who sent me testifies on my behalf" (John 8:18). The image of Jesus and the Father as co-witnesses to each other before humankind has been little developed in Christian theology, but might well be considered for such development. The mutual witness of Father and Son might be part of what is signified by the Paraclete, an important image of God to stimulate reflection not only on human experience of God but reflection as well on the reality of inalienable human rights: not derived from human consensus but from the gift of the One of whom we say, "As God is my witness."

The well-told tale of Susanna and the elders, from the Greek additions to the Hebrew and Aramaic text of the Book of Daniel, corresponds neatly with the gospel story of the woman caught in adultery, but also fits in with the alternative gospel. The central figures are neither the delectable Susanna nor the lecherous elders but the upright and clear-sighted youth Daniel, whose name means "God is my judge." Susanna, falsely accused of adultery by the elders who wished to entice her into sin, appealed to God to vindicate her: "O eternal God, you know what is secret and are aware of all things before they come to be; you know that these men have given false evidence against me. And now I am to die, though I have done none of the wicked things that they have charged against me!" (Dan 13:42–43). God sent his judgment through the youth Daniel, who brought about justice by entrapping those who had entrapped Susanna, separating them and revealing the inconsistency in their testimony as to the place of the alleged adultery. Daniel's style of interrogating the elders would never stand up in a court of law today, beginning as it did with sharp vituperation of the elders. But Daniel's courtroom technique achieved a just reversal of Susanna's condemnation. "The whole assembly raised a great shout and blessed God , who saves those who hope in him" (Dan 13:60). Jesus had no Daniel to defend him before his contemporaries, Jewish and Roman, except the Spirit-Paraclete who vindicated him at last.

TUESDAY OF THE FIFTH WEEK OF LENT
Readings: Numbers 21:4–9; John 8:21–30

The custom of veiling in mourning not only statues but even the cross in Catholic churches during what used to be called, in an older liturgical pattern, Passiontide (the fifth and sixth weeks of Lent), might have made sense when the cross was gloriously empty, a dramatic symbol of the resurrection. But when, from the Middle Ages on, the cross portrayed, sometimes quite graphically, the sufferings of the crucified Savior, veiling it for nearly two weeks and then unveiling it on Good Friday made less sense. Today's Liturgy of the Word unveils the cross as the sign of our healing or salvation.

The first reading narrates the curious tale from the period of Exodus of how the people of Israel were punished in the desert for their complaining by an infestation of "poisonous serpents" (Num 21:6), very possibly scorpions or some virulent skin disease characterized as burning in its effects (shingles?). When the people repented of their complaining, the Lord instructed Moses to reverse the effects of the serpent attack by making a bronze image of such a serpent: "Set it on a pole; and everyone who is bitten shall look at it and live" (Num 21:8). Is it too modern to see this as an exercise in confronting the source of one's discontent—burning desire concretized in complaining—and, with God's help, overcoming it?

The evangelist John saw the mounting of the bronze serpent as an image of the overcoming of all human selfishness in the mystery of the cross. "Just as Moses lifted up the serpent in the wilderness, so must the Son of Man be lifted up, that whoever believes in him may have eternal life" (John 3:14–15). This image returns implicitly in the gospel reading for this Lenten weekday: "When you have lifted up the Son of Man, then you will realize that I am he, and that I do nothing on my own" (John 8:28). More literally, the Greek of this verse states simply that "you will realize that I am." It is precisely in the human annihilation of Jesus as our fellow mortal that we are enabled to realize finally his total identification with Yahweh, the One who alone can say of himself "I AM."

WEDNESDAY OF THE FIFTH WEEK OF LENT
Readings: Daniel 3:14–20, 91–92, 95; John 8:31–42

Many Jews, both in ancient times and today, bear both Jewish and Gentile names. Thus in the New Testament we meet John Mark, whose Hebrew name *(Yochanan)* precedes his Latin name (*Marcus,* as in Mark Antony and Marcus Aurelius), as well as Paul (*Paulus,* Latin for "small") whose Hebrew name was Saul. The custom of renaming Jews who lived in a Gentile environment may derive from the Hellenization policies of the Seleucid Greek tyranny in early second century B.C. Syria. The

Book of Daniel, a fictional exhortation to Jewish fidelity in such a situation, projects the custom back into the sixth century B.C., when Daniel and his faithful Jewish companions in the court of Babylon—Hananiah, Mishael and Azariah—were renamed by the chief chamberlain of King Nebuchadnezzar as Belteshazzar, Shadrach, Meshach and Abednego (Dan 1:7), thereby exchanging theophoric Hebrew names for names of uncertain but decidedly non-Yahwistic Babylonian significance.

Name changes did not necessarily entail changes in faith, and the three companions of Daniel-Belteshazzar survived their Gentile trial very well as narrated in the first reading today. Refusing to worship an idol set up for the purpose of enforcing a Babylonian national cult, Shadrach, Meshach and Abednego found themselves condemned to a burning furnace. Their faith in Yahweh remained steadfast, no matter what happened to them: "If our God whom we serve is able to deliver us from the furnace of blazing fire and out of your hand, O king, let him deliver us. But if not, be it known to you, O king, that we will not serve your gods and we will not worship the golden statue that you have set up" (Dan 3:17–18). Inspecting the furnace to which he had condemned them, Nebuchadnezzar found to his dismay not only the three young Jews "unbound, walking in the middle of the fire, and they are not hurt" but also a mysterious fourth figure who "has the appearance of a god" (Dan 3:92).

The presence of Yahweh with his beleaguered faithful in the Babylonian furnace parallels the powerful presence of Jesus with his people in their struggles to bear witness to their faith in him. In the gospel passage from John, Jesus assured "the Jews who had believed in him" (John 8:31) that he would be for them the Son of God who delivers from slavery to the big lie and to sin: "If you continue in my word, you are truly my disciples; and you will know the truth, and the truth will make you free" (John 8:31–32). The audience seems to change at this point and those who heard Jesus utter these words seem no longer to be his believing Jewish disciples but a more hostile group. Resenting the implication that they as descendants of Abraham needed to be set free, these contemporaries of Jesus challenged him on his role as bearer of liberating truth. Jesus retorted that they had forfeited their freedom through sin, later evidenced by their plotting to kill him (John 8:40): "Everyone who commits sin is a slave to sin. The slave does not have a permanent place in the household; the son has a place there forever. So if the Son makes you free, you will be free indeed" (John 8:34–36). Jesus walks with us in the fiery furnace of a sometimes antagonistic world and offers us divine rescue more complete than that of any one with the appearance of a god: "I came from God and now I am here" (John. 8:42).

THURSDAY OF THE FIFTH WEEK OF LENT
Readings: Genesis 17:3–9; John 8:51–59

Not only Jews and Christians see Abraham as their father in faith but Muslims as well, although the frequent Qur'anic references to Abraham have more in common with certain extrabiblical Jewish traditions than they do with the biblical narratives. The reinterpretation in the New Testament of stories about Abraham from the Book of Genesis reaches its most dramatic highpoint in the gospel passage for this Lenten weekday when the fourth evangelist presents us with Jesus claiming an anteriority to the patriarch that could only be divine: "Very truly, I tell you, before Abraham was, I am" (John 8:58). The reaction of his audience in this Johannine narrative indicates that they regarded his words as a blasphemous claim to identity with Yahweh, who alone could utter the divine name "I AM WHO I AM" (Exod 3:14).

The first reading takes us to the third major narrative of Abraham's call in Genesis, the one usually said to be derived from priestly traditions more concerned with progeny than with land in the divine promise: "This is my covenant with you: You shall be the ancestor of a multitude of nations....I will make you exceedingly fruitful; and I will make nations of you" (Gen 17:4, 6). For the Jews in the period of priestly rule after the Babylonian exile, many of them living in diaspora throughout the Middle East and the Mediterranean world, descent from Abraham meant more than possession of the land of promise, although hope for possession of that land, free from foreign domination, did survive: "I will give to you, and to your offspring after you, the land where you are now an alien, all the land of Canaan, for a perpetual holding; and I will be their God" (Gen 17:8).

Jesus promised to his disciples something different from either Abrahamic progeny or the sovereign possession of land, the principal elements of the old covenant. "Very truly, I tell you, whoever keeps my word will never see death" (John 8:51). This solemn asseveration (more literally, "Amen, amen, I tell you,") accompanies the most central enunciations of the new covenant in John's Gospel. We are bidden to commit ourselves in faith, to say our "Amen," as Jesus did, who is called in the Book of Revelation "the Amen, the faithful and true witness" (Rev 3:14). This mutuality of faith, the exchange of a divine and a human "Amen" in Jesus, constitutes the new covenant. The promise of endless life eclipses (but does not completely eliminate) the promises of land and progeny and unites all of humankind in a new chosenness transcending that of Abraham. In this new chosenness it is Jesus who keeps the covenant for us: "I do know him [God the Father] and I keep his word. Your ancestor Abraham rejoiced that he would see my day; he saw it and was glad" (John 8:55–56).

FRIDAY OF THE FIFTH WEEK OF LENT
Readings: Jeremiah 20:10–13; John 10:31–42

Jeremiah's life was never easy. Called by God to be "a fortified city, an iron pillar, and a bronze wall, against the whole land" and promised by God that "I am with you...to deliver you" (Jer 1:18–19), the prophet often found himself quite vulnerable, even suspecting that he had been abandoned by the Lord: "You have enticed me, O Lord, and I was enticed" (Jer 20:7). The head of the Temple police, Pashhur, son of Immer, hounded Jeremiah for prophesying against the Temple as the guarantee of Jerusalem's safety from foreign conquest. For the first time in his prophecy Jeremiah named the nation that would humiliate Jerusalem and its officialdom: "You, Pashhur, and all who live in your house, shall go into captivity, and to Babylon you shall go" (Jer 20:6). The first reading comes from a passage shortly after the narration of Jeremiah's conflict with Pashhur and his feeling of abandonment by God. Despite his feelings, the prophet puts his faith in the Lord: "The Lord is with me like a dread warrior; therefore my persecutors will stumble, and they will not prevail" (Jer 20:11).

On this Friday one week before Good Friday, the gospel passage portrays Jesus, also a critic of the Temple and its priesthood, surrounded by hostile onlookers. Seeming to take up from yesterday's gospel passage when his listeners in the Temple "picked up stones to throw at him" (John 8:59), today's passage in fact comes from two chapters later in the gospel, just after Jesus has proclaimed in the vicinity of the Temple that "the Father and I are one" (John 10:30). This statement went even further than the proclamation of his eternal anteriority to Abraham (John 8:58). Jesus provoked the guardians of the Temple and its symbolization of the separateness of God and humanity to attempt to stone him, thus invoking against him the legal punishment for blasphemy (Lev 24:11–16). Asking the mob why they were trying to kill him, Jesus was told quite openly that "you, though only a human being, are making yourself God" (John 10:33).

At this point Jesus engaged in a somewhat recondite reading of Psalm 82, by modern exegetical standards, in order to justify a broader use of the terms God or gods than was normal. By the time of Jesus the original context of the Psalm in a largely poly-theistic setting had been forgotten. In that ancient environment Yahweh, the God of Israel, was depicted as a hero dethroning the rival gods of the surrounding nations for their malfeasance in office as judges of humanity: "How long will you judge unjustly and show partiality to the wicked?...I say: 'You are gods, children of the Most High, all of you; nevertheless, you shall die like mor-tals, and fall like any prince'" (Ps 82:2, 6–7).

By the time of Jesus, however, the Psalm was understood as a denunciation of unjust human judges, judges who nonetheless were addressed as gods because they exercised a divine responsi-bility. "Is it not written in your law, 'I said, you are gods'? If those to whom the word of God came were called 'gods'—and the scripture cannot be annulled—can you say that the one whom the Father has sanctified and sent into the world is blaspheming because I said, 'I am God's Son'?" (John 10:34–36). Jesus asked his listeners to judge from his works—the signs of God's pres-ence in Jesus to heal and save—whether he was performing divine works or not, "so that you may know and understand that the Father is in me and I am in the Father" (John 10:38). Good Friday, one week away, looms on the horizon as his listeners "tried to arrest him again," but his hour had not yet come and so "he escaped from their hands" (John 10:39).

SATURDAY OF THE FIFTH WEEK OF LENT
Readings: Ezekiel 37:21–28; John 11:45–57

Whenever there has been acrimony in American political life, almost inevitably some candidate, even a former fomenter of acrimony, emerges as the champion said to be able to "bring us together again." A great deal of imagery derived from family counseling colors such political rhetoric, some of it justifiable but much of it bogus, trying to replace the push and pull of political life with something more akin to group therapy. The prophet Ezekiel, living at a time when the worldly fortunes of the Jewish state were at their lowest ebb, used different imagery for what the Lord would do after the Babylonian exile for the divided and dispersed Northern and Southern Kingdoms of Israel and Judah. Israel, smashed by the Assyrian Empire in 721 B.C., and Judah, conquered by the Chaldeans in 587 B.C., Ezekiel compared to two separate wooden sticks which the prophet was to "join...together into one stick, so that they may become one in your hand" (Ezek 37:17). This the prophet did so that his listeners would ask him what Yahweh wanted him to symbolize. "Never again shall they be two nations, and never again shall they be divided into two kingdoms" (Ezek 37:22). That hope for a united Jewish nation settled on its ancestral land has survived even to modern times.

The integrity of the Jewish nation and its settlement in the Palestinian region of Roman Syria, severely challenged by the time John's Gospel was being edited in the decades after the Roman destruction of the Temple, struck the Sanhedrin, normally divided between antipathetic Pharisees and Sadducees, as one of the problems posed by Jesus. "What are we to do? This man is performing many signs. If we let him go on like this, everyone will believe in him, and the Romans will come and destroy both our holy place and our nation" (John 11:47–48). John the evangelist dramatizes the situation by having Caiaphas, one in a series of high priests heavily dependent on Roman imperial patronage, speak to this issue. "You know nothing at all! You do not understand that it is better for you to have one man die for the people than to have the whole nation destroyed" (John 11:49–50). The evangelist interprets the words of Caiaphas in terms of prophecy significant for Christians, Jewish and Gentile alike, although the historical high priest would have been speaking like this in view of the threat to Jewish national survival posed by messianic uprisings against Rome.

John's Christian interpretation of the words attributed to Caiaphas resonates with an entire theology of the significance for all humanity of the death of Jesus: "He did not say this on his own, but being high priest that year he prophesied that Jesus was about to die for the nation, and not for the nation only, but to gather into one the dispersed children of God" (John 11:51–52). The Gospel and the Epistles of John at least partly reflect a period in church history in Asia Minor when divisions among Christians—very possibly one house church pitted against another—threatened the unity of the new people of God. For the evangelist John the unity of Christ's flock was of paramount importance: "I have other sheep that do not belong to this fold. I must bring them also, and they will listen to my voice. So there will be one flock, one shepherd" (John 10:16). On this final Saturday before Holy Week the unifying power of the redemptive death of Jesus stands out in bold relief.

Chapter 7

THE BEGINNING OF
HOLY WEEK

PASSION (PALM) SUNDAY

Gospel Readings before the Palm Procession:
(A) Matthew 21:1–11; (B) Mark 11:1–10 or John 12:12–16;
(C) Luke 19:28–40
Readings at Mass: Isaiah 50:4–7; Philippians 2:6–11;
(A) Matthew 26:14–27:66; (B) Mark 14:1–15:47;
(C) Luke 22:14–23:56

THE GOSPEL READINGS
FOR THE PROCESSION WITH PALMS

The Roman liturgical renaming of Palm Sunday as Passion Sunday (a name formerly attached to the fifth Sunday in Lent) has never really caught on, at least in English. The enactment of the procession with palms may be more elaborate in some settings than in others, but the distribution of blessed palm on this Sunday is common to many Christian churches, or the distribution of blessed pussy willow in places like Byzantine Russia, where a tropical growth like palm is more difficult to obtain. Each of the four gospels has its unique description of the entry of Jesus into Jerusalem. Matthew and Luke, as usual, take the lead in the A and C cycles respectively; in the B cycle either Mark or John may be read.

(A) For **Matthew**, the messianic entry fulfills prophetic expectation. "This took place to fulfill what had been spoken through the prophet, saying: 'Tell the daughter Zion, Look, your king is coming to you, humble and riding on a donkey, and on a colt, the foal of a donkey'" (Matt 21:4–5). Writing, at least partly, for a Jewish-Christian community, Matthew was anxious to point out the continuities between the deeds of Jesus and the expectations of the Jewish people in the Second Temple period for deliverance from foreign oppression. The words attributed to "the prophet" seem to derive from two diverse passages in the prophetic literature.

The first comes from the third voice in the Isaiah tradition, a postexilic writer a bit disappointed with the results of Jewish return to Jerusalem after the Babylonian exile. Nevertheless, Third Isaiah held out hope for a renewal of the marriage between Yahweh and Jerusalem, imaged as "daughter Zion," the feminine personification of the Temple mount and the city that surrounded it: "The Lord has proclaimed to the end of the earth: Say to daughter Zion, 'See, your salvation comes'" (Isa 62:11).

The second prophetic source comes from a later author, the second major writer in the Zechariah tradition: "Rejoice greatly, O daughter Zion! Shout aloud, O daughter Jerusalem! Lo, your king comes to you; triumphant and victorious is he, humble and riding on a donkey" (Zech 9:9). The humble self-presentation of Zechariah's king may derive, in some sense, from the original rather humble entry of Solomon into Jerusalem "on King David's mule" (1 Kgs 1:38), or the use of other lowly mounts by the preroyal leaders of Israel (see Gen 49:11, Judg 5:10; 10:4). Third Isaiah's expectation of Yahweh as Jerusalem's divine savior and Zechariah's hope for a lowly human messiah combine in Matthew's portrait of Jesus entering the Jewish capital.

(B) [1] **Mark's** story of the entry into Jerusalem strikes some significant themes taken up in his later account of the passion. Jesus, almost as majestic and omniscient in Mark's narrative of the passion as in John's, instructs his disciples to precede him to the next village on the way toward Jerusalem where they "will find tied there a colt that has never been ridden" (Mark 11:2).

This young beast of burden they were instructed to untie and bring back for his mount: "The Lord needs it" (Mark 11:3).

Entering Jerusalem mounted on a colt, Jesus stirred up (perhaps unwillingly) enthusiasm for a new Son of David, enthusiasm expressed in words derived from Psalm 118:25–26. "Hosanna! Blessed is the one who comes in the name of the Lord! Blessed is the coming kingdom of our ancestor David! Hosanna in the highest heaven!" (Mark 11:9–10). Whereas Matthew's editorial addition to the Psalm quotation of the combined citation of Third Isaiah and Second Zechariah suggested the coming of both God and a human messiah in Jesus, Mark's narrative seems to hew more closely to the merely human messianic expectations of the Jerusalem crowd, expectations that were to be disappointed within a week, as the passion narrative demonstrates.

(B) [2] **John's** succinct account of the entry of Jesus into Jerusalem is very similar to the other more detailed narratives in the expectations of Jesus attributed to the Jerusalem crowd: "Hosanna! Blessed is the one who comes in the name of the Lord—the King of Israel" (John 12:13). Coming in the name of the Lord could simply imply a certain delegation by Yahweh for Jesus, something that could be said of a purely human messiah. Or, more typically of John, it could also imply that Jesus comes bearing the divine identity, plunged into the divine reality of the name spoken to Moses in the burning bush: "I AM WHO I AM" (Exod 3:14). Somewhat secondarily the crowd in John's Gospel thinks of Jesus as the king of Israel, not so much Davidic (as in Matt 21:9 and Mark 11:10) as divine.

(C) **Luke** begins his account of the entry into Jerusalem, as do Matthew and Mark, with the business of obtaining the mount on which Jesus would ride. When the disciples acclaim the mounted Jesus with the words of Psalm 118, Luke includes in their words a phrase asserting the royal character of Jesus: "Blessed is the king who comes in the name of the Lord!" (Luke 19:38). It is as if Luke wished to combine Matthew's insistence on the arrival of Yahweh and Mark's insistence on the arrival of the human messiah. Immediately thereafter the Jerusalem crowd added to their messianic acclaim from Psalm 118 words that seem to echo the angelic celebration after the annunciation of the birth of Jesus to the shepherds: "Glory to God in the highest heaven, and on earth peace among those whom he favors" (Luke 2:14). For Luke's Jerusalem crowd the acclaim is expressed more succinctly: "Peace in heaven, and glory in the highest heaven" (Luke 19:38).

Luke notes that "some of the Pharisees in the crowd said to him, 'Teacher, order your disciples to stop'" (Luke 19:39). The double assertion of the identity of Jesus with Yahweh and his role as the messiah of the Jews offended Pharisee orthodoxy and threatened the worldly security of the Jewish state within the Roman Empire. At the entry into Jerusalem Luke suggests that Jesus threw such caution to the winds. "If these were silent, the stones would shout out" (Luke 19:40).

But the crowds are fickle, fond of you when you seem powerful and forgetful of you when your luck runs out. Jesus may have meant his entry into Jerusalem mounted on a colt to reflect Zechariah's vision of a humble future messiah (Zech 9:9). The crowds are seldom happy with such leadership; it implies something very painful for them in their followership.

THE FIRST AND SECOND READINGS

The first and second readings at Mass on every Palm (Passion) Sunday remain the same, the Third Song of the Servant of Yahweh from Second Isaiah, and Saint Paul's unforgettable quotation of an early church hymn—possibly a composition by Paul—in the Epistle to the Philippians. The first and second readings for this Passion Sunday direct our attention to the dramatic passion narratives from Matthew, Mark and Luke.

The depiction of the Servant of Yahweh in four poetic compositions of Second Isaiah underlines the various gospel portraits of Jesus as the victim of persecution. Jesus preferred the role of Suffering Servant sketched by Second Isaiah to the messianic pretensions wished on him by his more ambitious disciples. The Suffering Servant of Yahweh, speaker in the first reading excerpted from Second Isaiah, voices the sentiments of every victim of obscene power in whatever century or clime. The third song contrasts the Servant with all self-serving and self-saving leaders: "I was not rebellious, I did not turn backward. I gave my back to those who struck me, and my cheeks to those who pulled out the beard; I did not hide my face from insult and spitting" (Isa 50:5–6). Jesus modeled himself on the Servant of Yahweh, even when his disciples would have wished he had taken King David for his hero. Jesus chose being human and poor and a victim of our history of sinful inhumanity.

In what seems to be a first-century Christian hymn quoted by Paul in this Sunday's second reading, the Messiah Jesus is said not to have considered equality with God "something to be exploited" (Phil 2:6). The translation loses some of the concreteness of the original Greek word, *harpagmos*. The Greeks called the bundle they associated with misers *harpagmos*, "spoils" or "plunder." What Paul means, more concretely, is that Jesus did not cling to his divine status in the way a bag person holds on to his or her worldly possessions.

More clear minded than any one of us obsessed with self-worth and private property, Jesus saw through every self-centered delusion and was willing to die for us, stripped of all that was his and nailed to a cross. He renounced every possession, even the possession of his own identity with God. Because of such voluntary self-abasement, Paul's hymn tells us, God "highly exalted him" (Phil 2:9). Few of us can emulate completely such divine renunciation of self. For becoming the most abject of human beings, a crucified criminal, God gave Jesus "the name that is above every name" (Phil 2:9), Paul's hymn proclaims. Stripped naked for our grasping selfishness, Jesus made a breakthrough for selfless humanity into the endless realm of Godhead.

THE SYNOPTIC PASSION NARRATIVES

(A) **Matthew's** account of the passion and death of Jesus contrasts the death of Jesus with that of Judas. Jesus died at the hands of sinners; Judas took his own life, overwhelmed with guilt at the enormity of his betrayal. Judas spoke the first words in the account of these parallel passions and deaths: "What will you give me if I betray him to you?" (Matt 26:15). The self-seeking character of Judas, his interest in money, stands in stark dialectic with the portrait of Jesus, who knew but did not reveal the identity of his betrayer.

Three times in Matthew's passion story Jesus used a phrase of pregnant ambiguity. Each usage underlines an important stage in the narrative. In the first instance, Judas at the Last Supper joined the other disciples in asking whether he would be the one to betray Jesus. Unlike the others, however, who addressed Jesus as "Lord" (Matt 26:22), Judas used the title normally employed by the faithless in Matthew's Gospel, "Rabbi" (Matt 26:25). To his inquiry Jesus replied with studied reserve: "You have said so" (Matt 26:25). The others could interpret this noncommittal expression as they pleased. Jesus and Judas alone realized its true significance. Jesus did not accuse Judas of treason; he left that ugly accusation to the betrayer himself. Without pointing a finger, however, Jesus warned Judas that it would be better not to have been born.

The next time Jesus employed the same expression is narrated in the trial of Jesus before Caiaphas, the high priest. After refusing to answer the charge that he had threatened to destroy the Temple and raise it up again in three days, Jesus finally broke his silence when the high priest adjured him to admit whether or not he was "the Messiah, the Son of God" (Matt 26:63): "You have said so" (Matt 26:64). Jesus spoke thus, aware that Caiaphas, like Judas, understood these messianic terms in this-worldly terms. The love of Judas for money, even a paltry sum like thirty pieces of silver, and the love of Caiaphas for power, even the puppet high priesthood controlled by the Romans, provide the gloomy shadows around the radiant figure of Jesus submitting to death with an almost stoic majesty. "From now on you will see the Son of Man seated at the right hand of the Power and coming on the clouds of heaven" (Matt 26:64). Caiaphas pounced on this declaration, derived from the vision of Daniel (Dan 7:13), as blasphemy, and he tore his garments in symbolic grief.

The third usage of this ambiguous answer (its tense changed) comes up in the trial of Jesus before Pontius Pilate. Betrayed by a disciple and handed over to the colonial authorities by the high priest of his own people, Jesus confronted in Pilate the representative of Roman domination. "Are you the King of the Jews?" the anti-Semitic Roman governor asked. "You say so" (Matt 27:11), Jesus quietly answered. For Pilate the question implied subversive action against Roman authority; for Jesus such kingship meant only coronation with thorns, mock homage, enthronement on a cross. In the supreme irony of this colonial drama, Pilate released to the mob an anti-Roman agitator, Barabbas, and crucified one with no such political ambitions.

Judas, Caiaphas and Pontius Pilate each played their parts in the drama that brought Jesus to the cross. Other figures, more sympathetically portrayed, entered into the action: Gentiles, diaspora Jews, Pilate's nameless wife, Simon the Cyrenian, the Roman centurion and his men who confessed, at the crucifixion, "Truly, this man was God's Son!" (Matt 27:54). Matthew wrote his Gospel precisely for a community of such diaspora Jews intermixed with Gentiles. Encouraging them in the late first century, Matthew gave them ancestors in the faith to sustain their hearts in a time of rejection by rabbinic Judaism and Roman officialdom.

(B) **Mark's** account of the passion contains in the narrative of the arrest of Jesus two verses unique to this Gospel that suggest symbolically a polar opposite to the messiah's self-renunciation. After noting that all the disciples of Jesus "deserted him and fled" (Mark 14:50), Mark goes on to mention, almost as an aside, that one nameless young man momentarily stayed with Jesus captive, only to flee eventually, and in considerable disarray. "A certain young man was following him, wearing nothing but a linen cloth. They caught hold of him, but he left the linen cloth and ran off naked" (Mark 14:51–52).

Scripture scholars have exercised their wits in trying to figure out who this young man was or what he signified. John Mark himself? A symbolic presentation of a baptismal candidate? A double of the "young man, dressed in a white robe" whom the women encountered in the empty tomb at Easter dawn (Mark 16:5)? We do not really know. All we have is the eloquent image of a young man (like the rich man of Mark 10:17–22) who followed Jesus part of the way to the cross, but not all of the way. The panic-stricken youth abandoned the scant dignity of his simple linen cloth and fled naked into the enveloping darkness of Gethsemane. He abandoned the one possession he had in order to save himself from the fate awaiting Jesus.

Two types of nakedness emerge as motifs in Mark's passion narrative: that of the frightened young man and that of Jesus, whose executioners "divided his clothes among them, casting lots to decide what each should take" (Mark 15:24). The Christian is offered a choice between types of nakedness. Go out of this life naked with Christ or naked with the fearful ex-disciple. There are, as they say, no pockets in a shroud, or, as Job put it, "Naked I came from my mother's womb, and naked shall I return there" (Job 1:21). We have no choice about finally keeping our possessions; the only choice we have is how we give them up. Consumerism has no ultimate future.

Mark's account of the passion reaches its highpoint with the earthquake and other phenomena that accompanied the last breath of Jesus. The Roman centurion speaks up for Mark's and Peter's Roman audience when he declares, "Truly this man was God's Son" (Mark 15:39). Mark had begun his Gospel with the definite assertion that it was "the beginning of the good news of Jesus Christ, the Son of God" (Mark 1:1). No mistaking the author's point of view after that opening. The point of Mark's Gospel, or of any gospel, is to win the listener or the reader over to the evangelist's point of view. The Roman centurion pointed the way for a Roman audience. God, who exalted Jesus and "gave him the name that is above every name" (Phil 2:9), can give you and me the pure gift of recognizing with that Roman centurion the Son of God in a man impaled on a cross.

(C) **Luke's** passion narrative centers, as does his Gospel more generally, on festive meals taken in common. A British anthropologist once wrote that eating is a biological necessity but feasting is not. If we're desperate enough, we will eat in any situation and with any *companion*, a word that derives from a Latin root denoting the sharing of bread. But those with whom we choose to feast are more limited. Commoners would never presume in a society with royalty to sit down to table with the king and queen. Even in democratic societies, those untrained in the elaborate etiquette of which utensil to use for which delicacy will shy away from formal banquets. Somewhere between eating and feasting lies the phenomenon called commensality, eating together as a sign of friendship, good will, reconciliation. In some cultural settings, shared tobacco (the peace pipe) or shared wine ("a cup of kindness") provide the symbolic expression for such commensality.

Jesus provoked scandal among his contemporaries in first-century Palestine by sharing the table of notorious violators of the Mosaic Law. The tax collector Levi "gave a great banquet for him in his house, and there was a large crowd of tax collectors and others sitting at table with them" (Luke 5:29). At dinner in the house of a Pharisee, Jesus encouraged a gate-crasher, "a woman in the city, who was a sinner" (Luke 7:37), and received from her the rites of hospitality denied by his somewhat niggardly host.

Jesus himself as host fed the multitudes with bread and fish (Luke 9:12–17) and urged the seventy-two disciples he sent on mission to accept the hospitality of peaceable hosts: "Remain in the same house, eating and drinking whatever they provide" (Luke 10:7). The best reception a host could give Jesus involved listening to his word, as the sisters Martha and Mary learned (Luke 10:38–42). Faithful servants of the absent Master who await his return will find themselves, to their surprise, treated as his guests: "He will fasten his belt and have them sit down to eat, and he will come and serve them" (Luke 12:37). Disciples of Jesus are urged to practice hospitality for the poor: "Invite the poor, the crippled, the lame, and the blind. And you will be blessed, because they cannot repay you" (Luke 14:13–14). Especially in Luke's Gospel, images of commensality abound.

The beginning of the end of that Gospel narrates how Jesus hosted his Last Supper for and with sinners: "I have eagerly desired to eat this Passover with you before I suffer....But see, the one who betrays me is with me, and his hand is on the table" (Luke 22:15, 21). The motley crowd of apostles argue among themselves "about which one of them was to be regarded as the greatest" (Luke 22:24) shortly after Jesus demonstrated the meaning of his living and his dying in terms of the broken bread and a shared cup. The uninvited sinful woman (Luke 7:37) earlier mentioned had more insight into the commensality offered by Jesus than did the future leaders of his church. Nevertheless, reconciliatory commensality was offered even to the ambitious disputants at the Last Supper: "I confer on you, just as my Father has conferred on me, a kingdom, so that you may eat and drink at my table in my kingdom" (Luke 22:29–30).

The commensal reconciliation of Jesus with sinners at the Last Supper did not stop sinners from betraying Jesus, denying knowledge of him, abandoning their role as his followers. It fell to a diaspora Jew from what is now Libya to pick up the cross and follow him: "As they led him away, they seized a man, Simon of Cyrene, who was coming from the country, and they laid the cross on him, and made him carry it behind Jesus" (Luke 23:26). Ironically, this stranger to the company of the disciples alone managed to respond to the call to take up the cross daily and follow Jesus (Luke 9:23). Without sharing in the Last Supper or any other meal with Jesus, Simon the Cyrenian may have found himself the only man among the women disciples within sight of the cross, at least in Luke's Gospel.

But there was one more sinful man to be offered the symbolic reconciliation of commensality at the Place of the Skull. Later Christian legend baptized this man Dismas and made him the patron saint of prisoners and thieves. His declaration of faith is unforgettable: "Jesus, remember me when you come into your kingdom" (Luke 23:42). The crucified Messiah did remember, inviting his fellow victim to share with him the delights of Paradise, the enclosed garden of the new creation where "God made to grow every tree that is pleasant to the sight and good for food" (Gen 2:9): "Today you will be with me in Paradise" (Luke 23:43). Even before the guests at the Last Supper, the good thief entered into the kingdom the Father had conferred on Jesus. He ate and drank at the Messiah's table beneath the fruit trees of Paradise.

MONDAY OF HOLY WEEK
Readings: Isaiah 42:1–7; John 12:1–11

Civil servants, prime ministers, aides, deacons and similarly named officials in church and state have in common their designation as people assigned to serve others. When they become mere bureaucrats, however, those who exercise power through holding one or another office, they often forget their role as servants. In ancient times, the servant was not always adequately distinguished from the slave. Jesus called on those who wanted to serve nothing but the cause of his crucified kingship to become figurative eunuchs (Matt 19:12), those who renounce the possibility of posterity and have no other cause to advance except God's.

The four songs of the Servant of Yahweh, high points of Second Isaiah (Isa 40:1–55:13), found their original context in the new concept of itself Israel came to in the wake of the Babylonian exile. With the Davidic kingship extinguished, the Jewish remnant reestablished in Judea—more cosmopolitan than they had been before their sojourn as exiles in Mesopotamia—began to think of Israel less in terms of Davidic or Solomonic splendor in a relatively circumscribed part of the eastern Mediterranean. Instead they began to realize that the Law given to the children of Israel could have an important moral significance as well for their Gentile neighbors. But a Servant of the Lord whose role it is to admonish others, including the Gentile neighbors of Israel, does not always have an easy path to follow.

The first song of the Servant of Yahweh, the first reading for this Monday of Holy Week, specifies that Yahweh has commissioned his Servant to "bring forth justice to the nations" (Isa 42:1) and that "the coastlands wait for his teaching" (Isa 42:4). The coastlands for the author of second Isaiah were the Gentiles near to Israel in the Mediterranean basin. Yahweh intended to enlighten these pagans through his Servant Israel: "I have given you as a covenant to the people, a light to the nations, to open the eyes that are blind, to bring out the prisoners from the dungeon, from the prison those who sit in darkness" (Isa 42:6–7).

The gospel reading from John shows Jesus not so much as a servant but as one served. In the household of Martha, Mary and Lazarus these friends of Jesus host a meal for him, possibly a celebration of the raising of Lazarus from the dead. In Luke's Gospel Martha was more famous as the one who served at table

(Luke 10:40), but in John's Gospel Mary shares the duties of hospitality in a rather extravagant fashion reminiscent of the hospitality exercised by the sinful woman in Luke's Gospel (Luke 7:37–38). "Mary took a pound of costly perfume made of pure nard, anointed Jesus' feet and wiped them with her hair" (John 12:3). Did Jesus, who washed the feet of his disciples a few days later (John 13:1–20), learn this role of servanthood from Mary of Bethany? Did Mary of Bethany learn it from Luke's sinful woman? We can only speculate. Jesus rebuked Judas who saw in Mary's extravagance only a waste of money that might have been spent on the poor (John 12:4–8). But there was a point to the objection raised by Judas. The church at its best has imitated the extravagance of Mary of Bethany and the extravagance of Jesus himself in pouring itself out on the poor whom we always seem to have with us as guests at our table, a reminder of Jesus whose feet were anointed at table in Bethany.

TUESDAY OF HOLY WEEK
Readings: Isaiah 49:1–6; John 13:21–33; 36–38

The prophet Jeremiah had made himself unpopular with patriots in Jerusalem in the years just before the Chaldean conquest in 587 B.C. of that remnant of Judea. Jeremiah knew from the beginning of his prophetic career that he had been called by God to deliver bad news, or at best, a bracing mixture of bad news with good news: "Now I have put my words in your mouth. See, today I appoint you over nations and over kingdoms, to pluck up and to pull down, to destroy and to overthrow, to build and to plant" (Jer 1:9–10). There were many times when Jeremiah regretted his call to be an unpatriotic prophet: "Whenever I speak, I must cry out, I must shout, 'Violence and destruction!' For the word of the Lord has become for me a reproach and derision all day long" (Jer 20:8).

Some people think that the memory of Jeremiah may have haunted the exiled Judeans and contributed to their understanding of the figure called the Servant of Yahweh in Second Isaiah. The first reading for this day of Holy Week evokes the image of a prophet called to deliver difficult words from God: "He made my mouth like a sharp sword, in the shadow of his hand he hid me; he made me a polished arrow, in his quiver he hid me away" (Isa 49:2). The prophet as God's secret weapon can hardly expect to have an easy time of it. But Second Isaiah as prophet did have some very good news to deliver to the returning exiles, that God intended "to bring Jacob back to him, and that Israel might be gathered to him" (Isa 49:5). But God wanted even better news to occupy the prophetic career of his Servant: "It is too light a thing that you should be my servant to raise up the tribes of Jacob and to restore the survivors of Israel; I will give you as a light to the nations, that my salvation may reach to the ends of the earth" (Isa 49:6).

Jesus knew at the Last Supper, in John's account of it, that Judas—one of those who shared his table fellowship—would betray him. Judas accepted from the hand of Jesus a morsel of the Passover supper, a symbol of shared love. But for Judas the morsel only accentuated the depths of his betrayal: "After he received the piece of bread, Satan entered into him" (John 13:27). Once Judas had left the table to begin the final stages of handing Jesus over to the authorities, the Gospel writer tells us that "it was night" (John 13:30).

But the night of Judas was streaked with the brightness of God's glory in Jesus. "When [Judas] had gone out, Jesus said, 'Now the Son of Man has been glorified, and God has been glorified in him'" (John 13:31). The humiliation of the despised Servant of Yahweh and the betrayal of Jesus by Judas and his desertion by Peter and the others ironically work greater glory for God than might have been achieved in the worldly triumph of Jesus over those who were plotting his demise. "If God has been glorified in him, God will also glorify him in himself and will glorify him at once" (John 13:32). But such closeness to God's glory can destroy mortal flesh. Jesus embraced that danger from the moment of his enfleshment in our midst.

WEDNESDAY OF HOLY WEEK
Readings: Isaiah 50:4–9; Matthew 26:14–25

Spy Wednesday takes its name from the activity (described in the gospel passage from Matthew) of Judas who betrayed Jesus to the authorities: "And from that moment he began to look for an opportunity to betray him" (Matt 26:16). In a sense, all of the disciples betrayed Jesus when they avoided possible arrest with him and only followed the events that transpired "at a distance" (Matt 26:58). Matthew tells us the exact price for which Jesus was betrayed: "thirty pieces of silver" (Matt 26:15). It is a peculiar irony that this was the rather modest sum prescribed in the Law to remunerate anyone whose slave had been gored by an ox (Exod 21:32) and also the paltry wages paid to the rejected shepherd in Zechariah 11:12. Jesus, the Good Shepherd who is also the Servant of Yahweh pierced for our salvation, was also valued at only thirty pieces of silver.

The third song of the Servant of Yahweh, Spy Wednesday's first reading, specifies the sufferings of the Servant who is the speaker: "I gave my back to those who struck me, and my cheeks to those who pulled out the beard; I did not hide my face from insult and spitting" (Isa 50:6). The physical abuse of the Servant does not discourage him, so reliant is he on God: "The Lord God helps me; therefore I have not been disgraced; therefore I have set my face like flint and I know that I shall not be put to shame" (Isa 50:7). Jesus identified himself with this Suffering Servant. Matthew and the other evangelists were undoubtedly influenced by the Servant songs when they described the blind-man's-buff cruelty meted out to Jesus by the Roman soldiers:

"After twisting some thorns into a crown, they put it on his head. They put a reed in his right hand....They spat on him, and took the reed and struck him on the head" (Matt 27:29, 30).

The third sorrowful mystery of the rosary dwells on the pathos of Jesus so abused. Infinite and compassionate majesty, sold for thirty pieces of silver, admits in sorrow that "it would have been better for that one [Judas] not to have been born" (Matt 26:24). On Spy Wednesday we can pray for all those who have so grieved the heart of God.

CHRISM MASS
(Celebrated with the bishop on Holy Thursday morning or earlier in Holy Week)
Readings: Isaiah 61:1–3a, 6a, 8b–9; Revelation 1:5–8; Luke 4:16–21

The annual Mass during which a diocesan bishop consecrates the oils used for baptism, confirmation, holy orders and the anointing of the sick is celebrated outside the Sacred Triduum, which begins on Holy Thursday evening, but ideally as closely as possible to those special liturgies in which the church recalls the central mysteries of our faith. Generally speaking, the main celebrant of this Mass is the bishop of the particular diocese joined by the priests who serve with him. The locale is ordinarily the diocesan cathedral. All of these practices are intended to emphasize the unity of the presbyterium, the body of ordained elders (*presbyteroi*, from which Greek word derives the word *priests*) who serve in constant and close collaboration with the presiding local elder or overseer (*episkopos*, the Greek from which *bishop* derives).

The readings for the Liturgy of the Word on this solemn occasion all center on the significance of anointing or christening as a ritual of appointment: prophetic, priestly and royal. The first reading, probably a narrative of the call of the third major prophetic figure in the tradition of Isaiah, speaks of his anointing by "the spirit of the Lord God" (Isa 61:1). Unlike priestly anointing, designating its recipients as the ritual officiants of Israelite worship, this prophetic anointing consecrates the speaker to a life of social activism: "to bring good news to the oppressed, to bind up the brokenhearted, to proclaim liberty to the captives, and release to the prisoners" (Isa 61:1). The reading goes on to declare that priestly anointing has been bestowed on the people of God as a whole: "You shall be called priests of the Lord, you shall be named ministers of our God" (Isa 61:6).

The selection from the opening of the Book of Revelation emphasizes the role of Jesus as the Christ or Messiah (anointed one) who is "the ruler of the kings of the earth" (Rev 1:5). The royal and priestly status conferred on Jesus he has in turn shared with all of us, lay and clerical, making us "priests serving his God and Father" (Rev 1:6). Note that neither royal nor priestly anointing as an individual privilege of the elders or presbyters of the church is emphasized in either of the first two readings.

In the gospel passage taken from Luke, Jesus begins his preaching career in Nazareth, his hometown, by applying to himself the prophetic call narrative of Third Isaiah excerpted in the first reading: "Today this scripture has been fulfilled in your hearing" (Luke 4:21). In a fashion reminiscent of the boldly defiant prophet Jeremiah, renowned for his lack of Judean patriotism, Jesus went on to tell his fellow Nazarenes that his anointing to a prophetic calling would not particularly enrich them or benefit them.

At the chrism Mass the members of the presbyterate are called upon to renew their commitment to selfless service of the Christian community. These three readings all remind us that such selfless service is meant as a prophetic sign of single-hearted commitment to the work of God.

Chapter 8

THE SACRED TRIDUUM

HOLY THURSDAY
EVENING MASS OF THE LORD'S SUPPER
*Readings: Exodus 12:1–8, 11–14; 1 Corinthians 11:23–26;
John 13:1–15*

The Mass of Holy Thursday evening begins one prolonged
liturgy that only ends with the conclusion of the Easter Vigil
service before dawn on Easter Sunday. Thus the liturgy of the
evening Mass of the Lord's Supper does not end with a final
blessing, nor does the celebration of the Lord's passion on Good
Friday open or close like a Mass. The Easter Vigil on Holy
Saturday begins with blessing of the new fire but ends with the
traditional dismissal at the conclusion of Mass, accompanied by
an elaborate *Alleluia*. Ideally all of us are invited to participate in
this integrated triduum or three-phase celebration of the
Passover of the Lord.

The first reading for the Mass of the Lord's Supper, taken
from the Book of Exodus, details how the Passover meal should
be prepared and served. The blood of the young male sheep or
goat (generically referred to as a lamb) was to be put "on the two
doorposts and the lintel of the houses in which they eat it" (Exod
12:7). Those blood markings were to single out the Israelites in
Egypt and protect them from the vengeance of the Lord on their
Egyptian oppressors. "I will pass through the land of Egypt that
night, and I will strike down every firstborn in the land of Egypt,
both human beings and animals; on all the gods of Egypt I will
execute judgments: I am the Lord. The blood shall be a sign for

you on the houses where you live: when I see the blood, I shall pass over you" (Exod 12:12–13).

Saint Paul, in the excerpt from his Corinthian correspondence that concerns the Lord's Supper, demonstrates his own rabbinic training in the formula he employs to hand on the apostolic tradition of what Jesus did and said with bread and wine on the eve of his death. "I received from the Lord what I also handed on to you" (1 Cor 11:23). He uses a very similar formula to introduce the apostolic traditions he received about the resurrection of Jesus (1 Cor 15:3). But Saint Paul insists in the account of the Lord's Supper that he received this tradition "from the Lord," rather than from Ananias, who was probably the first person who catechized him (Acts 9:10–19). This assertion demonstrates how seriously Paul took his first experience of the truth of the Christian mystery.

What Paul had personally experienced of Jesus as Lord was the total identification of Jesus with the Christian community Paul was persecuting: "I am Jesus, whom you are persecuting" (Acts 9:5). What Jesus did with bread and wine at the Last Supper, identifying himself on the night before his crucifixion and death with broken bread and a shared cup of wine, continues in his mysterious identification with his later disciples in their suffering for and with him. "As often as you eat this bread and drink the cup, you proclaim the Lord's death until he comes" (1 Cor 11:26). The crucifixion and death of Jesus on the first Good Friday, acted out prophetically in the manner of Jeremiah on the first Holy Thursday night, is repeated again and again whenever and wherever the disciples of Jesus suffer persecution for his sake. The eucharistic mystery is both the one sacrifice of Jesus and the supper foreshadowing it and continuing it. This reality underlies the liturgical continuance of the Mass of the Lord's Supper in the communion service (not a Mass) that concludes the Good Friday liturgy.

Although all three of the Synoptic Gospels (Matthew, Mark and Luke) give us detailed accounts of what Jesus did with bread

and wine at the Last Supper, John's Gospel does not, having treated at some length in the discourse on the bread of life (John 6:26–59) the double reality of that bread as the word of God proclaimed and accepted in faith and as the flesh and the blood of Jesus offered to us in meaningful concrete form. In his account of the Last Supper, John instead tells us how Jesus washed the feet of his disciples.

Only Luke's Gospel narrates the washing with tears and anointing of the feet of Jesus by the woman who had been a sinner who intruded herself into the banquet put on by Simon the Pharisee (Luke 7:36–50). Since Jesus and the other participants were reclining on couches at table in the Roman banqueting fashion, it was possible for the woman to enter from the rear of the dining couches and to weep over and then dry and anoint the feet of Jesus. The extraordinary self-abasement of the woman, a sign of her repentance for an unspecified sinful past, shocked Simon the Pharisee, who would have expected more reputable followers for a prophet. Jesus pointed out how close such a repentant sinner was to God. "Her sins, which were many, have been forgiven; hence she has shown great love. But the one to whom little is forgiven, loves little" (Luke 7:47).

In John's Gospel a similar gesture is performed not by a notorious sinner but by a close disciple of Jesus (along with her brother Lazarus and her sister Martha), Mary of Bethany (John 12:3). Very similar to the account of such an anointing by an anonymous woman in Mark (Mark 14:3–9) and Matthew (Matt 26:6–13), in each case the uneconomic extravagance of the act—rather than the self-abasement of the woman involved, as in Luke's story of the woman who had been a sinner—draws more attention in the other three gospels. In John's Gospel, Judas takes the blame for objecting to this extravagance (John 12:4); in Matthew and Mark the objection to the act seems more generalized among the disciples.

A few days later Jesus himself repeats at least some aspects of the gesture of Mary of Bethany, just as she seems to have repeated the gesture of Luke's woman who had been a sinner. But Jesus, poorer than any of the women who anointed his feet with oil, washes the feet of his disciples with simple water and dries them with a towel, an act very reminiscent of baptism. He performs this gesture of self-abasement and loving concern at a precise moment of insight he has attained: "Jesus knew that his hour had come to depart from this world and go to the Father. Having loved his own who were in the world, he loved them to the end" (John 13:1). The sinless one, who had nothing to repent for himself, took it on himself to offer himself as a sacrificial victim for sinners, first among them his disciples, apparently including Judas (John 13:2). "During supper, Jesus, knowing that the Father had given all things into his hands, and that he had come from God and was going to God, got up from the table, took off his outer robe, and tied a towel around himself. Then he poured water into a basin and began to wash the disciples' feet and to wipe them with the towel" (John 13:2–5).

Both the washing of the disciples' feet by Jesus (as narrated in John's Gospel) and the sacrificial sharing of his body and blood (as first described by Paul) center on the self-abasement of Jesus, his willingness to sacrifice himself for the sins of others. The water of the washing of the feet and the bread and wine of the Last Supper continue as the central sacramental symbols of Christianity: baptism and eucharist. In each of these sacraments Jesus pours himself out to save us from our sins.

GOOD FRIDAY
CELEBRATION OF THE LORD'S PASSION
Readings: Isaiah 52:13–53:12; Hebrews 4:14–16, 5:7–9; John 18:1–19:42

The Good Friday liturgy, in many ways a continuation of the Holy Thursday evening Mass, presents itself in three phases or

moments. It begins with a Liturgy of the Word that concludes with the ten magnificent intercessions for the needs of the church and of the world. The liturgy continues with the eloquent simplicity of the veneration of the cross and ends with a brief service of holy communion. From the opening prostration of the one presiding at the liturgy to the terse concluding prayer over the people, the atmosphere is one of solemnity combined with spareness. The church is not in mourning for the Lord whom we know to be risen and triumphant over death. But we are in mourning for our own sins, for our complicity in all the ways we crucify God's children.

Having heard the first three Servant of Yahweh songs in the daily liturgies of Monday, Tuesday and Wednesday of Holy Week, on Good Friday we hear the fourth and most elaborate of these songs. It starts off as a positive, even upbeat evaluation of the Servant by Yahweh himself: "See, my servant shall prosper; he shall be exalted and lifted up" (Isa 52:13). Immediately, with a jarring suddenness, we are presented with a very different and astonishing portrait of the Servant as one beaten and abused, "so marred was his appearance, beyond human semblance" (Isa 52:14). The Servant seems to be a victim of official abuse, "one from whom others hide their faces" (Isa 53:3). For what crimes is the Servant made to suffer? Not his own. "Surely he has borne our infirmities and carried our diseases; yet we accounted him stricken, struck down by God, and afflicted. But he was wounded for our transgressions, crushed for our iniquities" (Isa 53:4–5). We see the Servant slumped in a doorway, his face bruised and his body filthy, and we presume that he fell down there drunk or was deservedly beaten for his crimes. Only then do we discover that he was waylaid by officialdom looking to punish you and me for our misdeeds. "The Lord laid on him the iniquity of us all" (Isa 53:6). The crucial silence of Jesus before the superstitious questioning of Pilate (John 19:8–9) imitates that of the Servant: "Like a lamb that is led to the slaughter, and like a sheep that before its shearers is silent, so he did not open his mouth" (Isa 53:7).

Then, just as suddenly as the change after the opening verse, the mood changes back again to the positive evaluation of the Servant and his accomplishments: "When you make his life an offering for sin, he shall see his offspring, and shall prolong his days; through him the will of the Lord shall prosper.... The righteous one, my servant, shall make many righteous, and he shall bear their iniquities" (Isa 53:10, 11). Jesus identified himself so strongly with this portrait of the Servant of Yahweh that he shunned the glorious messianic ambitions his disciples held on his behalf. Few passages from the Hebrew Bible are more central to the understanding Jesus had of himself.

The second reading comes from the Epistle to the Hebrews, an anonymous late first-century theological treatise included in the New Testament. This exhortation dwells principally on the meaning of the priesthood and sacrifice of Jesus, possibly as these mysteries were reflected upon in a Jewish-Christian priestly setting. The first of the two brief excerpts from which the second reading is composed dwells on our sharing a common humanity with Jesus as our high priest and intercessor with God. But the humanity of Jesus, unlike our own, is sinless and beyond the need for personal expiation: "We do not have a high priest who is unable to sympathize with our weaknesses, but we have one who in every respect has been tested as we are, yet without sin" (Heb 4:15). Despite his innocence of sin, Jesus our high priest knew the human fear of death, as the second excerpt details: "Jesus offered up prayers and supplications, with loud cries and tears, to the one who was able to save him from death, and he was heard because of his reverent submission" (Heb 5:7). God, who heard the prayer of Jesus, did not exempt him from death, but brought him through death into a life-giving resurrection. "Having been made perfect, he became the source of eternal salvation for all who obey him" (Heb 5:9). One with God and one with us—true

God and true Man in the words of the creed—Jesus is the only priest of the new covenant, a perfect priest in whom God and humankind are united and reconciled. The conclusion of the first reading and the whole of the second reading make it clear that we are not mourning the death of Jesus on Good Friday but celebrating the saving effects of his passion and death.

The passion according to John depicts Jesus as the master of life and death, not a hapless victim of human iniquity. His mastery of his circumstances stands out vividly even when Judas and the soldiery come to arrest him in the garden. The evangelist insists, as in the narrative of the washing of the disciples' feet (John 13:1–3), that Jesus foreknew what was about to transpire. "Jesus, knowing all that was to happen to him, came forward and asked them, 'Whom are you looking for?'" (John 18:4). The question Jesus directs to his pursuers evokes a commonplace reply: "Jesus of Nazareth" (John 18:5). Precisely at this moment of apparently pedestrian communication, the next words of Jesus—suggesting that he is using the divine name—strike terror into the hearts of those who have come to arrest him. "Jesus replied, 'I am he.' Judas, who betrayed him, was standing with them. When Jesus said to them, 'I am he,' they stepped back and fell to the ground" (John 18:5–6). Usually translated, as here, "I am he," the New Testament Greek lacks the last pronoun, imitating the ordinarily unutterable name of God in Hebrew: "I AM WHO I AM" (Exod 3:14). It was for such apparent blasphemies (John 8:58) that the religious authorities wanted to arrest Jesus. And yet, in the darkness of the garden, some of the band surrounding Judas may have feared that what Jesus claimed for himself was true.

Whereas Jesus proclaimed his oneness with God in the "I AM" so typical of this Gospel, Peter admitted his frail and sinful humanity in his triple denial of his discipleship to Jesus: "I am not" (John 18:17, 25; see also 18:27). John the Baptist, at the beginning of this Gospel, had denied in similar terms that he was the messiah, Elijah or the prophet (John 1:20, 21), but the "I am not" in that case sprang from deeply honest humility, not craven fear. While Peter is denying his discipleship, Jesus testifies openly before Annas and Caiaphas, representing the Roman-dominated high priesthood: "I have spoken openly to the world; I have always taught in synagogues and in the temple, where all the Jews come together. I have said nothing in secret" (John 18:20).

The trial before Pontius Pilate, Roman procurator in Judea between A.D. 26 and 36, is dealt with at great length in John's Gospel (John 18:28–19:15). A protégé of Sejanus, the Jew-hating *eminence grise* of Tiberius Caesar, Pontius Pilate had gone to some lengths during his tenure in Jerusalem to offend the Jews, whom he, like his protector, despised. Trying to dismiss the obviously inner-Jewish religious charges brought against Jesus, Pilate told the accusers of Jesus to "judge him according to your law" (John 18:31). Only then did Pilate come to realize that the Jewish antagonists of Jesus wanted something more than they could accomplish as a subject people: "We are not permitted to put anyone to death" (John 18:31). The charge on which Jesus was to be executed was not a religious one of blasphemy (not a Roman concern) but a political one of defying Roman imperial rule by asserting for himself mundane kingship in Israel.

Pilate immediately took up this political charge with Jesus, first secluding himself and Jesus from the accusers: "Are you the King of the Jews?" (John 18:33). Romans had put down Jewish messiahs before and could do so again. The opportunity was open for Jesus to exculpate himself in private with Pilate, but instead he almost seemed to seek confrontation with the only authority who could exercise the *jus gladii* (the right to execute) in first-century Judea. He asked Pilate if he was putting the question about the meaning of his kingship out of his own curiosity, or based on the charges proffered by the accusers. In so querying Pilate, Jesus ignited the procurator's hatred of Jews: "I am not a

Jew, am I?" (John 18:35). Jesus began to speak with the procurator, very much a creature of this world, about a kingship not of this world. All Pilate wanted to know was the answer to the basic question: "So you are a king?" (John 18:37). Pilate discovered, to his administrative chagrin, that Jesus was making claim only to a kingship of truth. Many administrators have shared Pilate's cynical and dismissive attitude: "What is truth?" (John 18:38).

Ready to release Jesus on the trumped-up political charges against him, Pilate curried favor with the Jewish crowds by offering them, on the occasion of Passover, the amnestying of a political prisoner. Rather than choose the man Pilate referred to derisively as "the King of the Jews" (John 18:39), the crowds chose Barabbas, "a bandit" (John 18:40). The somewhat technical term used in Greek for Barabbas (*lestes*) suggests that he was not so much an ordinary bandit as an anti-Roman Jewish agitator. Furthermore, his name, Barabbas (Aramaic for "the father's son"), curiously echoes what Jesus had claimed for himself in relationship to God.

Apparently hoping to buy off the crowd with the physical punishment of Jesus, Pilate resisted their calls for crucifixion. In the process, the real charge against Jesus came out: "We have a law, and according to that law he ought to die because he has claimed to be the Son of God" (John 19:7). Not knowing what to make of such words emanating from monotheistic Jews, Pilate withdrew with Jesus once again. Superstitious like so many Romans, Pilate may have wondered what he was confronting in the so-called King of the Jews. "Where are you from?" (John 19:9), he asked Jesus, but Jesus did not answer. Jesus did not deny his divine sonship, even if the Roman military man's understanding of such sonship would have been polytheistic, at best. Interpreting the silence of Jesus as arrogance, Pilate insisted on his colonial authority. The majesty of Jesus emerges in full force in his reply to Pilate: "You would have no power over me unless it had been given you from above" (John 19:11). Pilate took the easy way out and returned to the unsubstantiated charge that Jesus had asserted a mundane kingship for himself, especially when the crowds suggested that Pilate's wavering indicated that he was "no friend of the emperor" (John 19:12). Behind this lies a technical term for the elite among Roman imperial administrators: *Amicus Caesaris* (Friend of Caesar). Pilate could not contain his rage with the Jews and taunted them with the charge that they were asking him to execute their king (John 19:15).

After the high drama of the trial before Pilate the Gospel of John plunges us into the details of the actual crucifixion of Jesus. Pilate's inscription on the cross, meant to annoy the Jews even further (John 19:21–22), remains on most crucifixes to the present day in Latin initials (INRI) signifying "Jesus of Nazareth, the King of the Jews" (John 19:19).

One detail unique to John's passion narrative is the presence of the mother of Jesus at the foot of cross along with her sister and another woman (both named Mary) and a mysterious male figure, the beloved disciple whose presence John's Gospel specifies five times (John 13:23; 19:26; 20:2; 21:7; 21:20) from the account of the Last Supper through the resurrection appearances. Who is this beloved disciple? At the end of John's Gospel he is said to be the witness "who is testifying to these things and has written them" (John 21:24), and so he is often identified with the evangelist John. The fact that his presence is only specified in the accounts of the suffering, death and resurrection of Jesus suggests that these events form the core of the Christian message, the saving death and resurrection of the Word made flesh. The mother of Jesus, never called Mary in John's Gospel, appears only twice in the Gospel, but there is a certain parallelism between her intervention at the marriage feast in Cana (John 2:1–12), where she urges the somewhat unwilling Jesus to perform "the first of his signs" (John 2:11), and her presence at the highpoint of his mortal life, when he

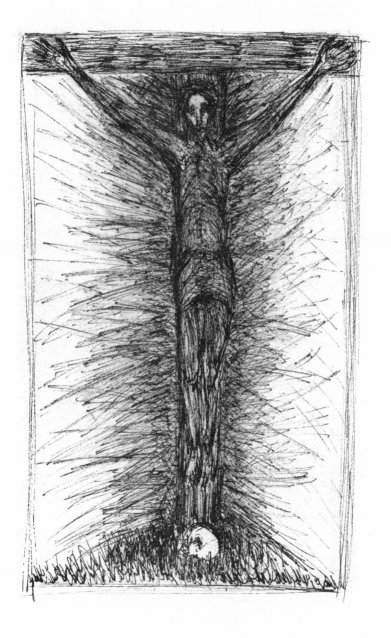

has finally reached his "hour" (John 2:4; see also John 12:23, 27; John 13:1). At this highpoint of the passion narrative, the mother of Jesus is given to the beloved disciple and the beloved disciple is given to the mother of Jesus. Much of Eastern and Western Christian devotion to the mother of Jesus as the model of the church and the mother of disciples flows from this passage in John's Gospel.

The Spirit, the water and the blood—a trinity of witnesses to the concrete, enfleshed reality of Jesus according to the First Epistle of John (1 John 5:6–8)—appear first in the account of the actual death of Jesus on the cross. The Gospel describes rather oddly the last breath of Jesus, although the New Revised Standard Version translates the words blandly: "He bowed his head and gave up his spirit" (John 19:30). More literally, the oddness of Greek phraseology suggests that Jesus, having bowed his head, "handed over the Spirit." The careful reader or listener may recall this phrase one chapter later in the account of the first resurrected appearance of Jesus to the eleven: "'As the Father has sent me, so I send you.' When he had said this, he breathed on them and said to them, 'Receive the Holy Spirit'" (John 20:21–22).

Shortly after the Gospel narrates the last breath of Jesus, it insists, against any merely spiritual reinterpretation of the Word made flesh, that "one of the soldiers pierced his side with a spear, and at once blood and water came out" (John 19:34) The Gospel writer's original audience may have been tempted to proto-Gnostic reduction of Jesus to a fleshless and bloodless being. The details of the death of Jesus on the cross are meant to counter that temptation to make Jesus so different from you and me. We hear the testimony of the beloved disciple to the fleshly concreteness and availability of God in Jesus: "He who saw this has testified so that you also may believe. His testimony is true, and he knows that he tells the truth" (John 19:35).

HOLY SATURDAY
THE VIGIL OF EASTER

Readings: (1) *Genesis* 1:1—2:2; (2) *Genesis* 22:1–18; (3) *Exodus* 14:15—15:1; (4) *Isaiah* 54:5–14; (5) *Isaiah* 55:1–11; (6) *Baruch* 3:9–15, 32—4:4; (7) *Ezekiel* 36:16–28; (8) *Romans* 6:3–11; (9) *[A] Matthew* 28:1–10; *[B] Mark* 16:1–7; *[C] Luke* 24:1–12.

Technically speaking, the Vigil of Easter belongs to the Easter season, but it looks backward and forward, a liminal night of mysteries, baptismal and eucharistic. The Easter Vigil expresses the primal liturgical experience of the Christian community. The Vigil—ideally stretching throughout the hours of night until dawn—begins in darkness with the Service of Light: the blessing of the new fire outside the church, the blessing and lighting of the Easter candle from the new fire and the solemn procession into the darkened church building with the Easter candle, from which all other candles are lit. An extraordinary encomium of the Easter candle is sung by a deacon in which the joy of the church over the resurrected triumph of Christ our Light is proclaimed. Then follows a Liturgy of the Word in which as many as nine readings may be read, or as few as five. But the account from Exodus of the Israelites' crossing of the sea in their escape from Egypt must always be read. After reflecting on these readings, in many ways the final prebaptismal catechesis of the catechumens, the participants in the liturgy proceed to the Liturgy of Baptism, normally the baptism of adults. This is usually the case in the newer churches of the Third World, where there are often many adult catechumens. The fourth and final phase of the Vigil service is the Liturgy of the Eucharist that completes the Sacred Triduum.

(1) *Genesis* 1:1—2:2. The primeval creation, imaged as the result of God's creative word spoken on six consecutive days, reflects a prescientific mind-set, a three-tiered universe of the fir-

mament overarching the earth with the underworld *(Sheol)* underpinning it. In the midst of this marvelous creation, God made the human being as the only image of the divine permissible in the anti-iconic Israelite tradition. Approving of everything so created, but especially of the male and female human image of the divine, "God saw everything that he had made, and, indeed it was very good" (Gen 1:31). On the Vigil of Easter, when catechumens are being ushered into the new creation through baptism, we look forward to a restored humanity made possible by Jesus, the new Adam who is the ultimate "image of the invisible God, the firstborn of all creation" (Col 1:15).

(2) Genesis 22:1–18. Primeval creation is followed by primeval sacrifice, the fulfillment of obedience to God, no matter how incomprehensible the sacrifice demanded. The testing of Abraham is one of the most terrifying stories in the Hebrew Bible. Abraham, only given one heir through his wife Sarah, is then told to "offer him…as a burnt offering" (Gen 22:2). It was through this only son that Abraham had supposed that he would become "the ancestor of a multitude of nations" (Gen 17:4). Unable to comprehend what God intends, the aged father obeyed against all his human instincts, trusting that somehow God would work sense out of this conundrum, and God did just that, substituting for the boy Isaac a sacrificial ram. So close to Good Friday we cannot but recall that God did not exempt himself from the sacrifice he had once asked of Abraham, and through the sacrifice of God's only Son "we have redemption through his blood, the forgiveness of trespasses, according to the riches of his grace that he lavished on us" (Eph 1:7–8).

(3) Exodus 14:15—15:1. At every Easter Vigil this reading must be read. The *Exsultet*, the encomium sung after the lighting of the Easter candle, dwells on the original Exodus as the first example of God saving his people. The baptism normally performed at the Easter Vigil is the new covenant's passing through water into the Promised Land. The Egyptian bondage

escaped by the newly baptized is enslavement to the powers of this world, the iron-eyed gods of power, materialism and pride. Saint Paul reminds the Corinthians that "our ancestors were all under the cloud, and all passed through the sea, and all were baptized into Moses in the cloud and in the sea" (1 Cor 10:1–2). Not everyone lives up to the newness of life such baptismal Exodus entails, but the Easter Vigil gives each of us an opportunity to repent and to renew our baptismal promises.

(4) Isaiah 54:5–14. The prehistory of salvation extends back beyond the escape of the Israelites from Egypt through the waters. Second Isaiah recalls the days of Noah when God "swore that the waters of Noah would never again go over the earth" (Isa 54:9). The prophet on God's behalf promises never again to abandon his rescued people: "For a brief moment I abandoned you, but with great compassion I will gather you. In overflowing wrath for a moment I hid my face from you, but with everlasting love I will have compassion on you, says the Lord, your Redeemer" (Isa 54:7–8). The tenderness of God's words through Second Isaiah suggest to the catechumens approaching baptism that they too are the objects of God's special predilection, his saving love.

(5) Isaiah 55:1–11. The baptismal motif comes out particularly clearly in this second selection from the prophetic composition of Second Isaiah: "Ho, everyone who thirsts, come to the waters; and you that have no money, come, buy and eat! Come, buy wine and milk without money and without price" (Isa 55:1). The restored Israel of Second Isaiah's era, returned to Jerusalem from Babylonian exile, has been given a broader view of God's power to save, even to save Gentiles. "See, you shall call nations that you do not know, and nations that do not know you shall run to you, because of the Lord your God, the Holy One of Israel, for he has glorified you" (Isa 55:5). In the new covenant inaugurated in the dying and rising of Jesus, as Peter declares in the house of Cornelius, "God shows no partiality, but in every nation anyone

who fears him and does what is right is acceptable to him" (Acts 10:34–35).

(6) *Baruch 3:9–15, 32—4:4.* A little known Greek supplement to the Jeremiah literature of the Hebrew Bible, the Book of Baruch is attributed to the secretary of Jeremiah, but probably takes its origin at a much later period when Wisdom literature was being composed by Hellenistic Jews in Greek. The present selection is part of a hymn praising Wisdom, especially as it is to be found in the Torah or the Law of Moses. The catechumens presented with the commandments in the third week of Lent are now reminded not to forsake this "fountain of wisdom" (Bar 3:12).

(7) *Ezekiel 36:16–28.* The final Old Testament selection, taken from the prophecy of Ezekiel, dwells on the reason for Israel's dispersal among the Gentiles, the defilement of Israelite life with idolatry, and the reason for the Lord's redeeming Israel from this exile: "It is not for your sake, O house of Israel, that I am about to act, but for the sake of my holy name, which you have profaned among the nations to which you came" (Ezek 36:22). Vindicating the divine holiness by saving guilty Israel, the Lord promises a baptismlike cleansing of the Chosen People: "I will sprinkle clean water upon you, and you shall be clean from all your uncleannesses, and from all your idols I will cleanse you" (Ezek 36:25). The Epistle to the Hebrews picks up this imagery when it urges its readers to approach the sanctuary of God "with a true heart in full assurance of faith, with our hearts sprinkled clean from an evil conscience and our bodies washed with pure water" (Heb 10:22).

(8) *Romans 6:3–11.* The baptismal motifs in the Old Testament readings prepare us for Saint Paul's most direct treatment of the saving effects of this rite of entry into the Christian mystery. "Do you not know that all of us who have been baptized into Christ Jesus were baptized into his death? Therefore we have been buried with him by baptism into his death, so that, just as Christ was raised from the dead by the glory of the

Father, so we too might walk in newness of life" (Rom 6:3–4). The baptisteries in many ancient churches were entered by descending steps into a gravelike pool in which the baptismal candidate was submerged and then raised up to his or her new life in Christ, "united with him in a resurrection like his" (Rom 6:5). Having gone through this ritual death and resurrection, newly baptized Christians are urged to think of themselves as "dead to sin and alive to God in Christ Jesus" (Rom 6:11).

(9) The Gospel. Each year of the liturgical cycle has its own Easter Vigil gospel. All agree that the first witnesses of the risen Jesus were women, whose testimony Paul, following rabbinic tradition (distrustful of female evidence), did not cite (1 Cor 15:3–8).

Year A: Matthew 28:1–10. Matthew's account of two women coming to the tomb, a bit more developed than the narrative in the Easter Vigil Gospel of Mark, follows similar lines in depicting the first witnesses to the resurrection of Jesus to be "Mary Magdalene and the other Mary" (Matt 28:1), who had come to see the tomb. There, after experiencing an earthquake, they encountered an angel descending who rolled back the stone at the entrance of the tomb just as they arrived. Told by the angel that "he is not here; for he has been raised, just as he said" (Matt 28:6), they took up "with fear and great joy" (Matt 28:8) the angelic command to bring this unlikely good news to the male disciples. On the way to fulfill this duty they met the risen Jesus, who repeated the command that had been given to them: "Do not be afraid; go and tell my brothers to go to Galilee; there they will see me" (Matt 28:10).

Year B: Mark 16:1–7. The truncated conclusion of Mark's Gospel tells us that at least three women came to the tomb, "Mary Magdalene, and Mary the mother of James, and Salome" (Mark 16:1), with the intention of embalming the corpse of Jesus. Finding the stone at the entrance of the tomb rolled back, the women entered the tomb and there met a white-robed youth who announced to them the news of the resurrection: "Go, tell

his disciples and Peter that he is going ahead of you to Galilee; there you will see him, just as he told you" (Mark 16:7). Unlike the women in Matthew's account, Mark's women do not meet Jesus and do not bring the good news to the disciples (Mark 16:8), but the Easter Vigil excerpt from the Gospel of Mark leaves out this final and disappointing verse.

Year C: Luke 24:1–12. Luke has a slightly different cast of women who went to the tomb to embalm the corpse of Jesus: "Mary Magdalene, Joanna, and Mary the mother of James," as well as some unnamed "other women with them" (Luke 24:10). As in Mark, they came upon the tomb already opened but inside they encountered "two men in dazzling clothes" (Luke 24:4). These two men have more to tell them than the angel in Matthew and the white-robed youth in Mark: "Remember how he told you, while he was still in Galilee, that the Son of Man must be handed over to sinners, and be crucified, and on the third day rise again" (Luke 24:7). Hastening to share this good news with the eleven disciples, the women met with male disbelief: "these words seemed to them an idle tale, they did not believe them" (Luke 24:11). Peter went to the tomb and found it empty, as the women had testified, except for the burial cloths. This emptiness of the tomb did not bring him to resurrection faith, at least at that moment, but "he went home, amazed at what had happened" (Luke 24:12).

All three of these Synoptic Gospel narratives of the first experiences of the resurrection of Jesus prepare us for the Easter season, and especially its first week (and first three Sundays), when all the gospel readings feature resurrection appearances of Jesus.

Chapter 9

THE SAINTS OF LENT

Only two solemnities (Saint Joseph on March 19 and the Annunciation of the Lord on March 25) and one feast (the Chair of Peter on February 22) take priority over the weekday Lenten celebrations, although the saints may be commemorated in the opening prayer of Mass. The pastoral value of consistent Lenten catechesis with the readings set for each day of Lent probably outweighs the value of commemorating the saints, although the name day of a particular church or the patron of a diocese may deserve more attention in particular cases. There follow brief accounts of all the saints who could possibly have memorials within the days of Lent, between February 5 and April 13. Saints whose memorials occur during Holy Week are not commemorated. Even the Solemnity of the Annunciation, when it occurs in Holy Week, is transferred to the Monday after the Second Sunday of Easter.

FEBRUARY 5
SAINT AGATHA, VIRGIN AND MARTYR OF SICILY

Saint Agatha undoubtedly died a martyr's death, probably in the persecution initiated under the Emperor Decius (A.D. 251), but the stories of assaulted virginity associated with Agatha all seem to be late and fictitious. They read like an old movie serial in the style of *The Perils of Pauline*. Her Greek name (meaning "good"), and the fact that she probably came from either Palermo or Catania in Sicily, have caused her to be commemorated in the martyrologies of the Greek churches of the East and the Latin churches of the West. In art she is often represented with a plate on which she carries her breasts, which the legends say were cut away when she was tortured. Their resemblance to loaves of bread has led to the blessing of loaves of bread in church on this day in Sicily. Those who live near Mount Etna in Sicily invoke her aid against volcanic eruptions. Since bells are often relied on as indicators of coming volcanic eruptions, Saint Agatha is the patroness of bell founders.

FEBRUARY 6
SAINT PAUL MIKI AND HIS COMPANIONS, MARTYRS OF JAPAN

Francis Xavier, a companion of Ignatius Loyola, arrived in Japan as that country's first Christian missionary in 1549. Within the next half century the number of Christian converts increased and caused a reaction from military elements in the government, who suspected foreign designs on Japan in the growth of Christianity. In 1597 three Japanese Jesuits—the scholastic Paul Miki and the coadjutor brothers (originally lay associates of the Jesuits) John Soan and James Kisai—along with six non-Japanese Franciscan missionaries and sixteen Japanese laypeople and one Korean were crucified in Nagasaki as part of the first wave of persecution of Christians in Japan. From his cross Miki eloquently defended the possibility of being both Japanese and Jesuit. Imitating Jesus he extended his forgiveness to his persecutors, saying that his religion had taught him to forgive his enemies, including the emperor and all who had sought to kill him. The deaths of these martyrs took place on February 5, 1597. Hundreds of other Japanese martyrs died for their Catholic faith in the course of the early seventeenth century. So extensive was the persecution of the Church and the closure of Japan to outside influences that the surviving but secretive "Kirishitani," encountered by missionaries in Japan in the nineteenth century, found it difficult at first to recognize their spiritual kinship with the Catholic missionaries who came again to Japan after its reopening to the West.

FEBRUARY 8
SAINT JEROME EMILIANI, PATRON OF ORPHANS AND STREET CHILDREN

Jerome Emiliani (1481–1537) began his adult career as a soldier in the service of Venice, not always successful on the battlefield. His capture as a prisoner of war and his escape from captivity led to a change for the better in his Christian life. At the age of 37 he was ordained a priest and dedicated the rest of his life to the care of the marginalized. Tainted with plague himself in the year 1531, Emiliani recovered and gave himself over even more wholeheartedly to the founding of orphanages, hospitals and halfway houses for prostitutes trying to escape their exploitation. To respond to these needs he founded a congregation of priests popularly known as Somaschi, from their place of origin, Somascha. They called themselves, more evocatively, the Society of the Servants of the Poor. Emiliani died of a disease caught from the sick poor he was tending on February 8, 1537. Pope Pius XI declared Emiliani the patron saint of orphans and street children.

SAINT JOSEPHINE BAKHITA, LIBERATED SLAVE AND REFUGEE

Born in the Dar Fur region of what is today Sudan around 1869, the unlucky girl whose memorial coincides with that of Saint Jerome Emiliani was given the name Bakhita by Arab slavers who kidnapped her around 1877. The name in Arabic means "lucky," but the girl's good fortune was a long time coming. Eventually bought from her Arab captors by the Italian consul in Kordofan, Bakhita was taken as a teenager to northern Italy. Although slavery was illegal in the Kingdom of Italy at that time, she remained a slave for some more years until she was faced with the possibility of returning to Sudan with her proprietors. This she resisted mightily, bringing into her struggle to retain her freedom and remain in Italy the sisters who were instructing her in the faith, the Cannossian Daughters of Charity. Baptized and confirmed by the Cardinal Patriarch of Venice in 1890, nearly four years later she entered the novitiate of that congregation. Her witness to the evils of slavery and the redeeming love of Christ endeared her to many in northern Italy, where she died on February 8, 1947. She was beatified by Pope John Paul II in 1992 and canonized by him in 2000. At a time when slavery is once again being practiced in Sudan, Saint Josephine Bakhita's memory deserves the attention of a wide audience.

FEBRUARY 10
SAINT SCHOLASTICA, SISTER OF BENEDICT

Traditionally said to be the sister of Saint Benedict, Scholastica demonstrates that women as well as men were attracted to the religious life in common in the Latin Church of the West from the sixth century onwards. The most famous story about Scholastica and Benedict is the account of their last annual visit. When Benedict wanted to conclude their edifying conversation about the joys of heaven, Scholastica, to his annoyance, called on God to send such a tempestuous rainstorm that Benedict could not return to his monastery. They spent the rest of the night in their pious discourse, not without some grumbling by Benedict. Three days later Benedict is said to have known that Scholastica had died when he saw a dove alighting towards the heavens.

FEBRUARY 11
OUR LADY OF LOURDES

Bernadette Soubirous (1844–1879), an impoverished child of Lourdes in the southeast of France, experienced a series of eighteen visions over a six-month period in 1858, beginning on February 11. In these visionary experiences she conversed with the Virgin Mary in the half-French, half-Spanish dialect of the region. The message of Lourdes was no different from the message of Jesus: "Repent, and believe in the good news" (Mark 1:15). The simple village girl, not unlike the Virgin who had originally let God take flesh in our world, proved to be the instrument of proclaiming that good news in the cynical and world-weary France of Napoleon III. Apart from those six visionary months, Bernadette's life was fairly humdrum. As a nun in later years she suffered terribly from tuberculosis of the bone. The miraculous cures that others found at Lourdes she did not. Like the handmaid of the Lord with whom she conversed in vision, Bernadette conformed herself completely to Jesus as the suffering Servant of Yahweh.

FEBRUARY 14
SAINTS CYRIL AND METHODIUS,
PATRONS OF TRANSLATION

Ninth-century brothers and missionaries from Thessalonica (Saloniki) in northern Greece, Constantine (later, as a monk, renamed Cyril) and Methodius had become priests in Constantinople. The Byzantine emperor sent them as mature men to Moravia, a still-pagan part of what is the modern Czech Republic, to preach the gospel there. The local ruler, who had invited the Byzantine emperor to send missionaries, wanted Cyril and Methodius to do their preaching and the celebration of the Divine Liturgy in the local language. This they did with alacrity, thereby starting the creation of written Slavonic, the precursor of all Slavic literature. Denied the episcopal right to ordain by German bishops of the Latin rite, Constantine and Methodius went to Rome where Constantine-Cyril died as a monk on February 14, 869. Methodius was ordained an archbishop in Rome before returning to Moravia. More tension followed with the German bishops and Methodius had to return to Rome to vindicate himself. Cyril and Methodius serve not only as patrons of the vernacular liturgy and Bible translation but also, along with Saint Benedict and Saint Edith Stein, as patrons of Europe no longer divided into East and West.

FEBRUARY 17
THE SEVEN FOUNDERS OF THE SERVITES

The thirteenth century witnessed the efflorescence in Italy, especially, of several new religious congregations characterized as friars, part-time wandering monks who were, nonetheless, tied to firm bases from which they set out on their evangelical journeys and to which they returned. The Franciscans, Carmelites, Dominicans and Augustinians are among the most famous of these orders of friars. Less famous are the Servites (Servants of Mary), who originated with the banding together of seven merchants of Florence. Starting as a confraternity devoted to the Virgin Mary, they took up residence on a hill outside Florence. After 1240 they took on some of the characteristics of a religious order and moved into town to pursue their apostolic duties. The last surviving Servite founder, Alexis Falconieri, remained a brother all his life and died on February 17, 1310.

FEBRUARY 21
SAINT PETER DAMIAN, REFORMER
OF THE CHURCH

Peter Damian spent most of his life in northern Italy as a notable example of reformed monastic and clerical life in the eleventh century when those forms of life had fallen into considerable decay. An orphan who had been well educated by his clerical older brother, Damian, he took that brother's Christian name as something of a surname. Peter eventually found himself attracted by the austerities of a Benedictine community reformed in the Camaldolese tradition of Saint Romuald. Much better educated than the other monks, Peter was called upon to preach a rigorous monastic reform not only in his home monastery but also in others. Around the year 1043 Peter became abbot and his reputation for reforming zeal brought him to the attention of several popes who were trying to cope with problems among the diocesan clergy like simony and clerical marriage, both of which led to the dissipation of church property. Pope Stephen IX called Peter Damian away from his monastery in 1057 and forced him to become Cardinal Bishop of Ostia, a suburban diocese of Rome, on threat of excommunication if he refused. Peter Damian eventually persuaded one of Pope Stephen's successors to allow him to retire back to his original monastery, where he spent his last years as a simple monk. The popes still called on him from time to time to leave the monastery on a temporary basis to reform one or another diocese. Peter Damian died on the return journey from one such reforming mission on February 22, 1072.

FEBRUARY 22
THE FEAST OF THE CHAIR OF PETER
Readings: 1 Peter 5:1–4; Matthew 16:13–19

This curiously named feast combines what once were two separate celebrations, the Chair of Peter at Rome (January 18) and the Chair of Peter at Antioch (February 22), neither of which referred to a literal chair. It used to be said that the worst weather of the winter in the northern hemisphere occurred "between the two Chairs." In fact, the much older Feast of the Chair of Peter referred to the commemoration of Peter's coming to Rome to lead the Christian community there—to occupy the *cathedra* or authoritative teaching and pastoral see or seat of Rome—and it has been celebrated as such on February 22 since the fourth century. It may well have been placed on that date to compete with a pagan Roman feast on which the citizens of the imperial capital venerated their dead relatives and left food on their graves.

The first reading comes from the First Epistle of Peter. The author exhorts "the elders among you" (1 Pet 5:1) to continue Peter's work of tending "the flock of God" (1 Pet 5:2). The Petrine imagination was permanently affected by the charge given by Jesus to Peter in the final chapter of the Gospel of John: "Feed my lambs....Tend my sheep....Feed my sheep" (John 21:15–17). A good shepherd is a gentle shepherd, not a tyrant, and can expect his reward "when the chief shepherd appears" (1 Pet 5:4).

The gospel reading enshrines the commission Jesus gave to Peter at Caesarea Philippi: "You are Peter, and on this rock I will build my church, and the gates of Hades will not prevail against it" (Matt 16:18). Any pilgrim to Saint Peter's Basilica in Rome can read this passage in the cupola over the main altar of that magnificent structure. Below the main altar in the crypt were buried, sometime in the 60s of the first century, the bones of the very human shepherd, once a fisherman, to whom Jesus entrusted the role of servant leader in his community. The fisherman turned shepherd was to keep the door of the messianic assembly surrounding Jesus: "I will give you the keys of the kingdom of heaven, and whatever you bind on earth will be bound in heaven, and whatever you loose on earth will be loosed in heaven" (Matt 16:19).

FEBRUARY 23
SAINT POLYCARP, BISHOP AND MARTYR

Polycarp, whose name means "much fruit" and refers to John 15:5, was probably a Christian from infancy or youth. At his death (ca. A.D. 155) he claimed to have been a Christian for 86 years. His Johannine name may well support the strong tradition that he grew up as a member of the community of the beloved disciple. He eventually became bishop of the Christian community at Smyrna (modern Izmir in Turkey). By the second century tendencies towards Gnosticism—the hypersymbolic reinterpretation of the gospels in terms consistent with a debased neo-Platonism—had infected the Christian church and other religious communities in the eastern Mediterranean. Polycarp followed the Johannine tradition in repudiating such excessive spiritualization of the crucified and risen Jesus. Towards the end of his life Polycarp was arrested in a reaction against Christians in Smyrna. Refusing to apostatize, Polycarp was put to death in the amphitheater and his body burnt.

MARCH 3
SAINT KATHARINE DREXEL, TEACHER
OF MINORITY STUDENTS

Katharine Drexel, born in 1858 of a wealthy Catholic family in Philadelphia, inherited much of the family fortune on the death of her stepmother in 1883 and her father in 1886. Taking her cue from the Third Plenary Council of Baltimore (1884), Katharine wanted to devote her inheritance to the evangelization and education of Native Americans and African Americans. She sought the guidance of Pope Leo XIII in her quest for a congregation of sisters who would undertake this work alone; the pope challenged her to found such a congregation herself. After her initial training with the Sisters of Mercy, she and her first companions launched the Sisters of the Blessed Sacrament in 1891, taking over for this purpose a former Drexel vacation home. Mother Katharine Drexel traveled indefatigably throughout the United States founding dozens of schools on all levels for Native Americans and African Americans, the most famous of them being Xavier University, which she founded in 1915 in New Orleans. The Drexel family fortune helped to finance the beginnings of these institutions. Katharine Drexel, long infirm in her old age, died at the age of 96 on March 3, 1955.

MARCH 4
SAINT CASIMIR, PATRON OF WAR RESISTERS

Casimir (1458–1484), third of the thirteen children of King Casimir IV of Poland, grew up very much under the influence of his pious teacher, John Dlugosz. His father—a busy kingmaker in central Europe with his many sons—thought of promoting Casimir as a new king for Hungary when Casimir was only 15. The army accompanying the youth abandoned him on the road to Hungary and Casimir regretted cooperating in his father's imperial plans. Coming back to Krakow in disgrace, the hapless youth was exiled to a suburban castle of Dobzki. Something of a patron saint thereafter for war resisters, Casimir was also determined to live a life of celibacy. He died of tuberculosis when he was 26. So devoted was Casimir to the medieval Latin original of the hymn known in English as "Daily, Daily, Sing to Mary," that he asked to be buried with it in his coffin.

MARCH 7
SAINTS PERPETUA AND FELICITY, MOTHERS AND MARTYRS

Carthage in North Africa—a suburb of modern Tunis—produced vivid Christian saints and martyrs between the third and the fifth centuries A.D. In the year 203, during the persecution initiated by the emperor Severus, Vibia Perpetua and her slave, Felicity, along with some male companions (Revocatus, Saturninus, Secundulus and their catechist, Saturus) were jailed for their Christian faith, even though the first five were only catechumens. Both Perpetua and Felicity were pregnant at the time or had recently given birth. Perpetua's struggles with her pagan father, who tried to convince her to pity her newborn child and himself and renounce her faith, occupy much of the authentic testimonies about these martyrs. Eventually all but Secundulus, who died in jail, were exposed to the beasts in the Roman amphitheater at Carthage on March 7, 203. Both the Eastern and Western Christian churches preserve the memory of these two extraordinary women who come up for mention in the First or Roman Eucharistic Prayer.

MARCH 8
SAINT JOHN OF GOD, PATRON OF HOSPITALS

Born in Portugal in 1495, the man who eventually earned the sobriquet "John of God" began his adult career as a mercenary soldier in the service of a Spanish count. Lapsing from any active Catholicism in this period, John only came back to the practice of his faith when he was a man of 40. For a while he wandered about selling religious pictures and books (for which he is the patron of booksellers) before a period in which he went religiously mad and was institutionalized. John of Avila, a famous preacher and spiritual guide of sixteenth-century Spain, had much to do with calming the mad John and redirecting his religious energies towards the charitable care of the destitute sick. This John did for the rest of his life, earning the name "John of God" from the bishop of Tuy. A bit like Mother Teresa in modern times, John of God's work for the sick poor drew the admiration and generosity of the nobility in Spain at the time. When John died of exhaustion in the year 1550, they all came to his funeral. The Hospitaller Brothers of Saint John of God were not directly founded by John of God in his lifetime. Twenty years after his death, people inspired by his example founded this religious congregation dedicated to the care of the sick. Saint John of God is the patron saint of hospitals, those who work in them and those who suffer in them. He might also serve as the patron saint of those who have suffered mental illness and recovered.

MARCH 9
SAINT FRANCES OF ROME,
PATRON OF MOTORISTS

Francesca, the daughter of a noble family from the Trastevere district of Rome, found herself unwillingly married off at the age of 13 into another noble Roman family, the Ponziani. She soon discovered that she and her brother-in-law's wife, Vannozza, who lived in the same household, had both really wanted to be nuns. They resolved to make up for their somewhat forced marriages by spending their husbands' money on the care of the poor, and their husbands deserve canonization for continuing to finance their wives' many charities without complaint. The Ponziani suffered dramatic reversals in their fortunes because of the struggles for control of Rome between popes and anti-popes and their respective military forces in the early fifteenth century. Francesca and her sister-in-law continued their charities, wherever possible. Two of Francesca's children died young and after the death of the second, she began to see a childlike angel who seemed to guide her for the rest of her life. It is perhaps for this reason that Pope Pius XI made Frances of Rome the patron saint of car drivers, who are to keep their eye out for children crossing the road. On her feast day the redoubtable motorists of Rome come to the Church of Santa Francesca Romana near the Roman forum to have their cars blessed. Saint Frances, who as a widow founded and then joined a congregation originally dedicated to the care of the poor, died at Rome on March 9, 1440.

MARCH 17
SAINT PATRICK, BISHOP
AND PATRON OF IRELAND

Magonus Sucatus Patricius, to use the Latinate version of his name, was a youth of somewhat upper-class origins, a Romanized Christian Celt. Born towards the end of the fourth century on the western coast of Britain or the western coast of France, his designation as a patrician gave him what has become his name for later generation, Padraig in Irish or Patrick in English. Taken captive as a teenager by pagan Irish pirates raiding his hometown in the early fifth century, Patrick spent six years as a slave tending sheep in Ireland. The solitude of his forced labor stirred up in him the previously smoldering coals of his Christian faith. Escaping to his homeland, Patrick eventually felt called to return to his former captors as a missionary. After some clerical training, probably in France, he was ordained a priest and later a bishop to replace the short-lived first missionary bishop sent to Ireland, Palladius. The notable success of Patrick's missionary labors and the vigorous response they elicited from all classes in Ireland culminated in the foundation of a distinctly inculturated Irish tradition of Catholic Christianity, quite different in some ways from Catholic Christianity in other parts of Europe. It was different as well from the ultramontane Catholic piety that came to dominate Ireland in the nineteenth century when Catholic emancipation, after years of foreign religious and political repression, was effected. The late ice age rather than Patrick kept snakes out of Ireland; the legend that he used the trefoil shamrock to explain the Trinity is ahistorical and does no credit to his theology. His authentic *Confession* and the *Letter to the Soldiers of Coroticus* provide us with a more realistic portrait of this vigorous missionary.

MARCH 18
SAINT CYRIL OF JERUSALEM, PATRON OF ADVENTUROUS THEOLOGIANS

Cyril of Jerusalem (315–386) spent the last half of his life in and out of Jerusalem as the city's archbishop. The sixteen years he spent out of Jerusalem he had been exiled from his archdiocese by the machinations of his theological and ecclesiastical opponents, most notably Acacius, the bishop of Caesarea. Although Cyril has been accused of semi-Arianism, a milder version of the fourth-century heresy condemned at the Council of Nicea (325), he never held such views but was only reluctant to use the neologism *consubstantial* (*homoousios*, in Greek) to describe the relationship of Jesus with the Father. He might serve as a suitable patron saint for those in more recent times who have tried to frame theological questions in terms that differ from the usually accepted language of past formulations. Later generations have revered Cyril as orthodox and have especially admired and studied his *Catecheses*, the written remains of the instructions he gave catechumens in fourth-century Jerusalem.

MARCH 19
THE SOLEMNITY OF SAINT JOSEPH
Readings: 2 Samuel 7:4–5, 12–14, 16; Romans 4:13, 16–18, 22;
Matthew 1:16, 18–21, 24 or Luke 2:41–51.

All that can be said about Joseph, the husband of Mary and foster father of Jesus, must be based on what Matthew and Luke have to tell us in their respective gospels. Many legends have grown up to supplement these few details, none of them historically reliable. The infancy narratives, more theologically significant than they are historically verifiable, do give us some insights into the Christian mystery, and especially the Pauline doctrine of justification by faith apart from works of the Law (Rom 3:21), in the way they present the just man Joseph.

The first of the two possible gospels for this day tells us that Mary, betrothed to Joseph, "before they lived together...was found to be with child from the Holy Spirit" (Matt 1:18). According to the Law such a woman should have been stoned to death along with the father of her child (Deut 22:21–23). Joseph, Matthew tells us, "being a righteous man and unwilling to expose [Mary] to public disgrace" (Matt 1:19), had decided to end his betrothal to Mary quietly. There is a paradox involved in the declaration that Joseph was a righteous man and yet unwilling to expose Mary to the rigors of the Law. His righteousness was not that of the Pharisees, not even that of the Book of Deuteronomy or the Law of Moses. The foster father of Jesus is also the foster father of justification by faith, God's freely given vindication of those whom the Law would condemn. He was appointed in a dream by God's angel to name the child to be born Jesus, thereby taking on the legal paternity of the child. The name of the child, *Yeshua*, was interpreted to mean "Yahweh saves," and indeed it was through the instrumentality of Joseph that Mary was saved from false accusations and we are saved from true accusations: this *Yeshua* is the one who "will save his people from their sins" (Matt 1:21).

The alternative gospel reading from Luke features the final narrative in Luke's account of the origins of John the Baptist and Jesus, the story of the losing and finding of the child Jesus. His parents fulfilled the Law (Deut 16:5–8) by making the annual Passover pilgrimage to Jerusalem, but the twelve-year-old Jesus seemed to break the fourth commandment by staying behind in the Holy City without his parents' permission. Searching for him in the Temple after they had returned to Jerusalem, they found him studying the Law, "sitting among the teachers, listening to them and asking them questions" (Luke 2:46). Mary took the lead in questioning his behavior: "Child, why have you treated us like this? Look, your father and I have been searching for you in great anxiety" (Luke 2:48). Jesus did not accept the accusation of disobedience to parents, making a pointed reference to his real paternal origins: "Did you not know that I must be in my Father's house?" (Luke 2:49). Such bold claims to the Temple and to a special filial relationship with God brought Jesus to the cross, an apparent violator of the Law that kept God and human beings distinctly separate. But God vindicated Jesus as he had vindicated Mary. Joseph's graced holiness came to him as he struggled to live with both of these mysteries.

Both Matthew (Matt 1:1–16) and Luke (Luke 3:23–38) trace the Israelite and human ancestry of Jesus through Joseph, his foster father, each gospel pointing out the descent of Joseph from the royal line of David. The first reading features the prophecy of Nathan to King David in which he assured the king that his dynasty would survive his death and that of Solomon: "Your house and your kingdom shall be made sure forever before me; your throne shall be established forever" (2 Sam 7:16). In fact, of course, the House of David only survived David by a little less than four centuries, and in a very attenuated form at the end. The apparent failure of this absolute covenantal promise led to messianic expectations in Second Temple Judaism, hope for a revival of the Davidic line. Both the genealogies of Jesus in Matthew and Luke point out that the Davidic descent of Jesus is not a matter of natural descent but of adoption by Joseph.

The second reading, excerpted from Paul's Letter to the Romans, zeroes in on the doctrine of justification by faith. Abraham became the father of many nations not through the Law but "through the righteousness of faith" (Rom 4:13). A bit like Abraham, Joseph's fathering of Jesus was not the result of the law of nature or of Joseph's conformity to the Law of Moses but of God's gracious intervention. Joseph, like Abraham, also became "'the father of many nations,' according to what was said, 'So numerous shall your descendants be'" (Rom 4:18, citing Gen 17:5 and Gen 15:5). Not unsuitably Joseph was declared by Pope Pius IX the patron of the whole church, that vast assembly of God's children brought to birth by the grace poured out in Jesus, our elder brother.

MARCH 23
SAINT TURIBIUS OF MONGROVEJO, BISHOP AND REFORMER OF PERU

Turibius of Mongrovejo (1538–1606), a Spanish nobleman and pious Catholic from his childhood, trained in law and was given the dubious honor of a royal appointment to preside as a layman over the Inquisition in Granada. So well did he do in that position that he was appointed archbishop of Lima in Peru, even though he had never been to Peru and was not even a priest. Ordained both priest and bishop in quick succession, he was dispatched to Peru. There he found, to his dismay, that both the Spanish colonial administrators and clergy were vastly corrupt. From 1581, the date of his arrival in Peru, until his death on March 23, 1606, Turibius as archbishop of Lima set himself the herculean task of reforming Christian life in that country. He especially distinguished himself as a champion of the native population of Peru, the victims of rapacious Spanish colonialism.

MARCH 25
THE SOLEMNITY OF THE ANNUNCIATION OF THE LORD
Readings: Isaiah 7:10–14; Hebrews 10:4–10; Luke 1:26–38

Although March 25 has been called "Lady Day" in the English tradition and was generally accounted a feast of the Virgin Mary in times past, the official title of this solemnity concentrates more on what was announced, the virginal conception of the Lord Jesus, rather than on the one to whom the news of this conception was announced. But the mystery of the Annunciation cannot be contemplated except as an interchange of the divine and the human, God becoming one of us, and one of us being perfectly caught up in the mystery of God. All of this was achieved through the generous response to God in faith of a young girl from Nazareth.

The first reading from Isaiah comes from the narration of a series of signs given by God to the prophet at the time of the Syro-Ephraimite war in the late eighth century B.C. Isaiah had been commissioned by God to encourage the fearful King Ahaz (r. 735–715 B.C.) to trust that God would save Judah from its enemies, an unholy alliance of the Northern Kingdom (Ephraim) and the Syrians. The names of three children, all of them possibly children of Isaiah, were (in the first instance) to signify that "a remnant shall return" (*Shear-jashub:* Isa 7:3) and (in the third instance) that "the spoil speeds, the prey hastens" (*Maher-shalal-hash-baz:* Isa 8:3).

The name of the second child, not clearly the offspring of the prophet, is "God is with us" (*Immanuel:* Isa 7:14). The three

children's names in the context of the eighth-century Isaiah were meant to encourage the timorous king. "God is with us," the second child, would not have grown to the age of being able to "refuse the evil and choose the good" (Isa 7:16), according to Isaiah, before the lands of Ephraim and Syria would be overrun in 721 B.C. by the conquering armies of Assyria. Scripture scholars tell us that it is unlikely that the young woman pregnant with the second child was considered a virgin by Isaiah. The important element in the sign in Isaiah's original context was not the marital status of the mother but the name of the child, as in the other two instances.

Matthew's Gospel shifted our attention from the name of the child to the marital status of the child's mother. He writes of Mary's pregnancy "from the Holy Spirit" (Matt 1:18) that "[a]ll this took place to fulfill what had been spoken by the Lord through the prophet: 'Look, the virgin shall conceive and bear a son, and they shall name him Emmanuel,' which means 'God is with us'"(Matt 1:22–23). Faced with the unique newness of the virginal conception of Jesus, Matthew sought for some way to link this newness with something old and known.

The gospel reading from Luke does not cite the Immanuel passage from Isaiah. The angel Gabriel did, however, use other terminology typical of Old Testament "holy war" motifs when he addressed the Virgin Mary: "Greetings, favored one! The Lord is with you" (Luke 1:28). Thus had the angel of the Lord addressed Gideon when Israel's political and military hopes were at a very low ebb in a time of Midianite raids. Gideon's reply challenged God: "If the Lord is with us, why then has all this happened to us?" (Judg 6:13). Luke tells us that Mary "was much perplexed by his words and pondered what sort of greeting this might be" (Luke 1:29). What was a teenage girl of Nazareth to make of such a "holy war" greeting? The angel immediately used another phrase very common in "holy war" passages from the Old

Testament: "Do not be afraid" (Luke 1:30; see Exod 14:13 and 20:20).

This little girl from Nazareth was being asked to subject herself to something very fearful, potential disgrace and obloquy in the "holy war" God would begin with her mothering a child out of wedlock: "How can this be, since I am a virgin?" (Luke 1:34). The angel assured her, as in all "holy war" passages from the Old Testament, that God would win the battle against all human odds, as the Lord did for the people of the Exodus in the pillars of fire and cloud: "The Holy Spirit will come upon you, and the power of the Most High will overshadow you" (Luke 1:35).

The Epistle to the Hebrews concentrates our attention on the newly incarnate Jesus coming into the world through the womb of Mary, dedicating himself, not unlike his virginal mother, to absolute obedience to God. Quoting the Greek version of Psalm 40, the author puts into the mouth of Jesus words of self-sacrifice: "Sacrifices and offerings you have not desired, but a body you have prepared for me; in burnt offerings and sin offerings, you have taken no pleasure. Then I said, 'See, God, I have come to do your will, O God'" (Heb 10:5–7). The Solemnity of the Annunciation is a mystery of a war won by God, and by God alone.

APRIL 2
SAINT FRANCIS OF PAOLA, ASCETIC AND WONDER-WORKER

Francis of Paola (1416–1507), more a man of the Middle Ages than of the Renaissance, seems to have been oriented from his childhood in Calabria to a life of penitential rigor. At the age of 15 he retired to a hermitage and within a few years was joined by others. Modeling themselves somewhat on the Franciscans ("the lesser Brethren" or Friars Minor), Francis of Paola and his companions, more monks than friars, called themselves "the least Brethren" (the Minims, from the Latin *minimi*). The hermitage soon developed into a large church and monastery. The Minims were to observe a perpetual Lent, abstaining from all animal products. Francis established a considerable reputation as a prophet and miracle-worker, his fame spreading beyond Calabria and Italy. Louis XI, the dying king of France, invited him to his realm; Francis at first refused but eventually went on orders from the pope. Instead of healing the king he advised him to prepare for death. The son and successor of Louis XI, Charles VIII, and his successor, Louis XII, persuaded Francis not to return to Calabria. Francis of Paola died on Good Friday 1507 and was buried in France. Canonized in 1519, the saint was beyond feeling the indignity of what happened to his body after his death: Huguenots disinterred the body in 1562 and burned it.

APRIL 4
SAINT ISIDORE OF SEVILLE, BISHOP AND SCHOLAR

Isidore of Seville (560–636), a man of vast learning born of a Roman family settled in Spain, is generally considered to be the last of the Latin fathers of the church. The Spain in which Isidore lived and wrote had been overwhelmed by the invasions of the Visigoths, barbarians originating in what is today eastern Europe. Learning and writing seem to have been Isidore's reaction to the ruinous decay of Roman and Latin Spain. Ordained a priest and later a bishop, Isidore worked vigorously to convert the Visigoth rulers of Spain from their Arianism (the heresy condemned at the Council of Nicea in 325 that denied Jesus equal divine status with the Father) to orthodox Catholicism. He was also anxious to develop the Catholic Visigothic polity as an independent counterbalance to the Eastern Roman Empire based in

Byzantium. Isidore's intellectual interests were not confined to theology and related sciences. His encyclopedic *Etymologies* attempted to gather together in twenty small volumes a summation of all knowledge. His work was much studied in the Middle Ages throughout Europe. His histories of the barbarians are more important today, in some cases providing our only written source on these peoples.

APRIL 5
SAINT VINCENT FERRER, DOMINICAN PREACHER

Vincent Ferrer (1350–1419), a Dominican friar and preacher of considerable ability, lived and worked at a time of acute difficulty in the church, the Great Western Schism (1378–1417). Two and at one time three different men claimed to be the pope simultaneously. Vincent's repute as a preacher and miracle-worker has overcome the fact that he for many years backed and worked for two of the anti-popes based in Avignon, Clement VII and Benedict XIII. Welcomed at the papal court in Avignon as chaplain, Vincent during the pontificate of Benedict XIII grew disenchanted with the anti-pope, especially when Benedict refused to accept the growing theological consensus against the legitimacy of his position. After what may have been psychosomatic illness brought on by his discomfort in the papal court at Avignon, Vincent distanced himself from Benedict XIII by obtaining the anti-pope's commission to preach a reforming mission throughout much of Europe in the early fifteenth century. It is even claimed that he preached with some success in Muslim Granada and in the Jewish synagogue at Salamanca. Despite his patronage by Benedict XIII, Vincent eventually persuaded the king of Castile to withdraw his obedience from Benedict, an event that helped to spell the doom of the Avignon papacy. Vincent Ferrer died in France on April 5, 1419.

APRIL 7
SAINT JOHN-BAPTIST DE LA SALLE,
SPONSOR OF EDUCATION

John-Baptist de La Salle (1654–1719), born into a prosperous family in Rheims, showed an early interest in the priesthood and was ordained in 1678. Almost by accident he found himself inspired to do something about the appalling lack of education of poor boys first in Rheims but then more generally in France. For this purpose he gathered together in his own home some lay teachers, not all of whom took to the monastic daily order by which he wished them to live. Eventually finding suitable lay teachers, he gradually came to the conclusion that they should become professed religious brothers. To avoid any semblance of caste in what they came to call the Institute of the Brothers of the Christian Schools, de la Salle and his first companions decided that none of the brothers should seek ordination. The brothers inaugurated the practice of teaching in the vernacular rather than Latin and also promoted vocational education and even reform-school education for different clienteles. Jansenists and others opposed the education of those whom they considered lower class and unsuited for any education at all, but John-Baptist de la Salle and his brothers began what has continued down to the present day, a tradition of solid Christian and secular education made available even to the poor. John-Baptist de la Salle died on Good Friday, April 7, 1719.

APRIL 11
SAINT STANISLAUS OF KRAKOW, BISHOP
AND MARTYR, PATRON OF POLAND

Poland itself and many Polish people look to Stanislaus Szczepanowski (1030–1079) as their patron saint. As bishop of Krakow after 1072 he preached indefatigably and exerted himself in notable concern for the poor. The king at the time, Boleslaus II, seems to have had much in common with Herod Antipas. When other bishops did not have the courage to face up to Boleslaus, Stanislaus did, excommunicating him for the kidnapping and rape of the beautiful wife of one of his subjects. The king decided to defy the excommunication and entered the cathedral of Krakow only to find that the clergy within immediately suspended the service in progress on the order of Bishop Stanislaus. Pursuing the bishop to a small chapel outside Krakow, the king himself killed Bishop Stanislaus, leaving it to his attendants to butcher the bishop's corpse. The pope at the time, Saint Gregory VII (r. 1073–1085), a notable opponent of defiant monarchs, put Poland under interdict until the people rose up and overthrew Boleslaus II. Pope John Paul II, once the inheritor of Stanislaus as archbishop of Krakow, made his formerly optional memorial on April 11 an obligatory memorial.

APRIL 13
SAINT MARTIN I, LAST MARTYR POPE

Martin I (d. 655), the last pope to be martyred, had succeeded to the See of Peter in 649. The struggles between various theological factions, especially in the Christian churches of the East, had brought the Byzantine emperors to involve themselves in these controversies in the hope of unifying the Christian East, by this time challenged by the rise of Islam. The Arabs had already wrested Egypt and Syria (including the Holy Land) from Byzantine imperial control. Pope Martin and the bishops at the First Council of the Lateran held in Rome rejected the Monothelite explanation of the unity of Godhead and humanity in Jesus because it seemed to assert that Jesus only had a divine will and not a human will. But the Byzantine emperor was sponsoring this Monothelite doctrine in the hope of finding a theological compromise halfway between the Monophysitism (insistence that Jesus had only one nature, divine) typical of Syrian, Armenian and Egyptian Christians and the Chalcedonian doctrine of the hypostatic union of humanity and divinity in Jesus who is at one and the same time truly God and truly human. The Byzantine emperor Constans II had his agent in Italy arrest Pope Martin in 653 and bring him in chains to Constantinople. After much physical abuse Martin was tried before the senate in Constantinople and thrown into a jail with common criminals. Eventually banished to Crimea, Martin died there after many hardships in 655. Venerated by both the Byzantine Greek church of the East and the Western Latin church, this hero of the unity of Christ and of the unity of the church used to have his feast in the West on November 12, but in 1969 the date was changed to April 13, the day on which he is also venerated by the Byzantines, including those not in union with Rome.